Editor
Walter Kelly, M.A.

Editorial Manager
Karen Goldfluss, M.S. Ed.

Editor in Chief
Sharon Coan, M.S. Ed.

Creative Director
Elayne Roberts

Associate Designer
Denise Bauer

Art Coordinator
Cheri Macoubrie Wilson

Cover Artist
Denise Bauer

Product Manager
Phil Garcia

Imaging
Ralph Olmedo, Jr.
James Edward Grace

Publishers
Rachelle Cracchiolo, M.S. Ed.
Mary Dupuy Smith, M.S. Ed.

ACTIVITIES

for any

Spelling Unit

PRIMARY

Author

Betty Martin Fox

Teacher Created Materials, Inc.
6421 Industry Way
Westminster, CA 92683
www.teachercreated.com
©1999 Teacher Created Materials, Inc.
Reprinted, 2000
Made in U.S.A.
ISBN-1-57690-312-5

Teacher Created Materials

Table of Contents

Introduction

Activities for Any Spelling Unit is a collection and compilation of many enjoyable and meaningful activities to be used with spelling. Organized into a weekly format, the activities can be used either as in-class assignments or as homework assignments. The activities are designed to provide drill and practice not only as spelling skills but also for teaching alphabetical order, sentence structure, dictionary skills, letter and spatial relationships, language skills, following directions, coding skills, and developing responsibility.

Because of added pressures on today's curriculum, many experienced teachers have become increasingly frustrated with the lack of time devoted to spelling. Many of these same teachers have seen their students become better workers, scientists, mathematicians, and thinkers but have also seen how their students' spelling skills have declined. There just doesn't seem to be time to fit it all in! It is from this frustration and the realization of the need to incorporate spelling back into the curriculum that this book—*Activities for Any Spelling Unit*—has been developed.

The word listing for each week's activities has been left open for each teacher to adapt to his or her own classroom requirements, although the management section contains a targeted selection of lists (pages 119–137) from which to choose or supplement words for each lesson. The activities are designed to give you the flexibility either to use them daily in your classroom or to send them home for homework. Perhaps the most manageable method for many teachers will be to introduce the spelling unit and skills on Monday, send the activity sheet home with exercises to be completed as homework each night, and then have it all returned to school on Friday. The assignments, however, can be returned on a daily basis as well. The manageability of *Activities for Any Spelling Unit* as well as the students' increased success as spellers has been proven in the classroom.

Included is a sample of how the assignments might look upon completion and a sample letter to parents, giving helpful hints as to how the assignments can best be completed as homework.

You will notice that for ease of use the book has been divided into four sections—*Level One Activities* for easier lessons (lower primary), *Level Two Activities* for more challenging lessons (upper primary), *Specific Skills Activities* for appropriate skills lessons, and a *Management* section for additional forms and word lists for the teacher, including a glossary of language terms you may wish to send home as a "memory refresher" for parents.

We are confident that you will recognize that the activities in this book are practical and classroom-proven. We hope that you will find *Activities for Any Spelling Unit* time-saving, meaningful, flexible, and powerful as a teaching tool in your classroom program.

Letter to Parents

Dear Parents,

Your child will be bringing home a spelling activities sheet each Monday. The sheet will have the list of spelling words for the week as well as the homework assignments for each night. All the spelling activities will be collected at one time—on Fridays. This means that your child will need to keep all the assignments together at home until Friday. It is important, however, that the assignments be done one night at a time in order to adequately drill and review the spelling unit, rules, and lessons being covered.

Here are some tips that will help your child successfully complete the spelling activities assignments:

1. It is helpful to have a **good children's dictionary** that is on your child's reading level and has definitions, sentences, guide words, and phonetic spellings.

2. It is helpful to have at home a **homework folder** in which to store ongoing work.

3. It is helpful to do **one assignment each night**—that is, do not wait until Thursday to do all assignments.

4. It is helpful to glance over your child's homework each night to **check for spelling mistakes and understanding** of the skills.

5. It is helpful to **remind your child to take his or her spelling assignments back to school** on Friday.

Together, the class has already completed a week of spelling activities to model how the assignments are to be organized and completed. The attached sample can be placed in your child's homework folder to be used as a guideline for future assignments. Also attached to this letter is your child's spelling activities sheet for this coming week along with a helpful "refresher" glossary of language terms for your use in helping your child.

Thank you for your support.

_____

Teacher

Spelling Activities Sample

Name _____ **Date** _5-12-99_____

Monday

1. bird, bird, bIrd
2. birth, birth, bIrth
3. fir, fir, fIr
4. first, first, fIrst
5. sir, sir, sIr
6. stir, stir, stIr
7. birch, birch, bIrch
8. dirt, dirt, dIrt
9. firm, firm, fIrm
10. girl, girl, gIrl
11. shirt, shirt, shIrt
12. third, third, thIrd

Tuesday

1. I have a pet bird named Tweety.
2. My dog gave birth to 24 puppies!
3. I have a fir tree in my front yard.
4. She was born first in my family.
5. Excuse me, sir.
6. Please stir the soup, Honey.
7. birch
8. dirt
9. firm
10. girl
11. shirt
12. third

Wednesday

1. bird
2. birth
3. fir
4. first
5. sir
6. stir

Thursday

#					
1.	b	bi	bir	bird	
2.	b	bi	bir	birt	birth
3.	f	fi	fir		
4.	f	fi	firs	first	
5.	s	si	sir		
6.	s	st	sti	stir	

#					
7.	b	bi	bir	birc	birch
8.	d	di	dir	dirt	
9.	f	fi	fir	firm	
10.	g	gi	gir	girl	
11.	s	sh	shi	shir	shirt
12.	t	th	thi	thir	third

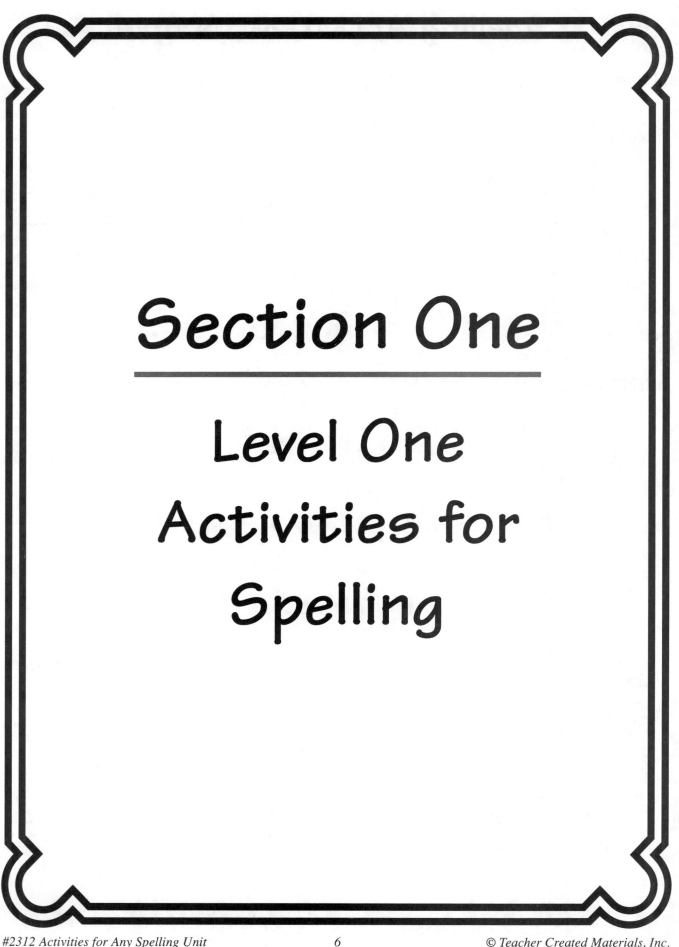

Section One

Level One
Activities for
Spelling

Activities for Spelling 【1】

☛ You will need a WORD SEARCH page for Thursday.

Name _____   *Week* _____

1. _____   6. _____
2. _____   7. _____
3. _____   8. _____
4. _____   9. _____
5. _____   10. _____

Monday ━━━━━━━━━━━━━━━━━━━━━━━

Write each spelling word in pencil, pen, and then marker.

Tuesday ━━━━━━━━━━━━━━━━━━━━━━━

• Write words 1–5 in "spelling stairs."

example:

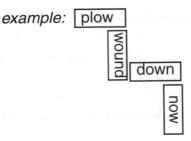

• Look up words 6–10 in a dictionary. Copy the sentence in which the word is used (be sure it is a sentence and not the definition).

Wednesday ━━━━━━━━━━━━━━━━━━━━━━

• Look up words 1–5 in the dictionary and copy the sentences in which the words are used.

• Write words 6–10 in "spelling stairs."

Thursday ━━━━━━━━━━━━━━━━━━━━━━━

Make a word search with your spelling words. Study for your spelling test.

Activities for Spelling 2

Name _____ Week _____

1. _____   6. _____
2. _____   7. _____
3. _____   8. _____
4. _____   9. _____
5. _____   10. _____

Monday

Write each spelling word three times. (Circle) your neatest writing for each.

Tuesday

Cut out letters from old newspapers and magazines to spell each of your spelling words. Glue the words onto your paper.

Wednesday

Use each of your spelling words in a sentence. Draw a ⬚box⬚ around each word with a different colored crayon.

Thursday

Make a chart with three columns—**Spelling Word**, **Same Beginning**, and **Same Ending**. Fill in your chart with the spelling words, a new word with the same beginning letter, and a new word with the same ending letter.

example:

Spelling Word	Same Beginning	Same Ending
read	(r)ain	san (d)

Activities for Spelling 3

Name _____ Week_____

1. _____   6. _____
2. _____   7. _____
3. _____   8. _____
4. _____   9. _____
5. _____   10. _____

Monday

Write each word as a "word wagon" by writing the beginning and ending letters on each wheel and using the word as the wagon bed.

example:

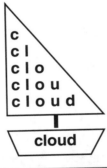

Tuesday

Write your spelling words in "sailboat" style.

example:

```
c
c l
c l o
c l o u
c l o u d
```
cloud

Wednesday

- Have an adult in the house dictate a sentence to you to write for words 1–5. (Circle) these spelling words.
- For words 6–10 dictate a sentence to an adult in the house to write down for you. Draw a [box] around these spelling words.

Thursday

Write your spelling words in alphabetical order from A–Z and then from Z–A.

example: A–Z: **aloud   cloud   found   mound   sound**

           Z–A: **sound   mound   found   cloud   aloud**

Activities for Spelling 4

Name _____   Week_____

1. _____   6. _____
2. _____   7. _____
3. _____   8. _____
4. _____   9. _____
5. _____   10. _____

Monday

Write each spelling word two times. Underline each vowel and circle each consonant.

example: **eleven   e⃝l⃝e⃝v⃝e⃝n⃝**

Tuesday

Write each spelling word normally and then again in code using the symbols below.

example: **word = △ ● ■ ÷**

a = ✳	b = △	c = ↑	d = ÷	e = □	f = ↓	g = ▼	h = ⊙	i = ✕
j = ○	k = ▽	l = ☆	m = ♥	n = →	o = ●	p = ⊡	q = ←	r = ■
s = ♡	t = ⊠	u = ▲	v = +	w = △	x = ✺	y = ★	z = ⊗	

Wednesday

Write a question for each spelling word. Circle the spelling word.

example: **Do you have (eleven) crayons?**

Thursday

Using the spelling words, write answers to each question you made up on Wednesday.

example: **I do not have (eleven) crayons.**

Activities for Spelling 5

Name _____ Week _____

1. _____ 6. _____
2. _____ 7. _____
3. _____ 8. _____
4. _____ 9. _____
5. _____ 10. _____

Monday

Write each spelling word in lowercase letters. Write it again in capital letters.

example: **between BETWEEN**

Tuesday

Write each spelling word in a "beginning letter blitz" by writing the word over and over to make the shape of the beginning letter.

example:

Wednesday

Write questions for each of your spelling words. Use correct dialogue form by including the name of who is speaking as well as commas, quotation marks, and question marks.

example: **Mary asked, "Do you sit between Ken and Debbie?"**

Thursday

Cut out letters from old magazines and newspapers and glue them onto your paper to spell out each of your spelling words.

Activities for Spelling 6

☛ You will need a WORD SEARCH page for Thursday.

Name _____   Week_____

1. _____   6. _____
2. _____   7. _____
3. _____   8. _____
4. _____   9. _____
5. _____   10. _____

Monday

Write your spelling words in ABC order from A to Z. Write them again in order from Z to A.

example: A–Z   **apple**   **car**   **forest**   **home**   **ink**   **listen**

Z–A   **listen**   **ink**   **home**   **forest**   **car**   **apple**

Tuesday

Write "tongue twister" sentences for each of your spelling words by using words that begin with the same letter as the spelling word.

examples: **<u>A</u>ndy <u>A</u>lexander <u>a</u>te <u>a</u>n <u>a</u>pple <u>a</u> while <u>a</u>go.**

<u>L</u>et's <u>l</u>isten to a <u>l</u>ovely <u>l</u>ullaby.

Wednesday

Write each spelling word and add "tag alongs" by using words that begin and end with the same letters.

example: w

i

l   i   s   t   e   n

a

p

Thursday

Use all your spelling words to make a word search. After filling it in, have a friend or family member circle the spelling words. You write down each word after they find them.

Activities for Spelling 7

Name _____ Week _____

1. _____   6. _____
2. _____   7. _____
3. _____   8. _____
4. _____   9. _____
5. _____   10. _____

Monday

Write each spelling word two times normally and then one time in all capital letters.

example: **ready   ready   READY**

Tuesday

Write a short paragraph using school as the topic. Have the paragraph take place at school, tell about school, or describe school. Include all of your spelling words in the paragraph somewhere.

Wednesday

Write each of your spelling words in "pea pods." Use each letter of the word as the peas of the pea pods. Group pea pods together with other "pea pods" having the same number of letters or "peas."

example:

Thursday

Write each spelling word. Think of another word that looks very similar to the spelling word and write it. Write your spelling word one more time.

example: **ready**   *read*   **ready**

Activities for Spelling 🎬 *8*

Name _____   Week _____

1. _____	6. _____
2. _____	7. _____
3. _____	8. _____
4. _____	9. _____
5. _____	10. _____

Monday ────────────────

Write each spelling word two times in pencil and one time in pen.

Tuesday ────────────────

Write spelling words 1–5 normally and then again in code using the symbols below:

example: **word** = △ ● ■ ÷

a = ✳	b = △	c = ↑	d = ÷	e = □	f = ↓	g = ▼	h = ⊙	i = ✕
j = ○	k = ▽	l = ☆	m = ♥	n = →	o = ●	p = ⊡	q = ←	r = ■
s = ♡	t = ⊠	u = ▲	v = +	w = △̇	x = ✾	y = ★	z = ⊗

Wednesday ────────────────

Use each of your spelling words in a separate question. Draw a box around each spelling word with a different colored crayon.

example: **Do you** |live| **in the United States?**

Thursday ────────────────

Write each spelling word. Then look up each word in the dictionary and write the guide words from the page on which you found each spelling word. (Guide words are the first and last words on each dictionary page and are written in **boldface** type at the top of each dictionary page.)

example: **word**   guide words = **wool/work**

Activities for Spelling 9

Name _____   Week_____

1. _____   6. _____
2. _____   7. _____
3. _____   8. _____
4. _____   9. _____
5. _____   10. _____

Monday

Write each spelling word. Write each word again using capital letters for vowels and lowercase letters for consonants.

example: **open   O p E n**

             closed   c l O s E d

Tuesday

Dictate a sentence for each spelling word to a parent or friend. Have that person write your sentences down. Go back and (circle) each spelling word with a crayon or pen.

Wednesday

Write each spelling word one time normally and one time in word triangles.

example:

Thursday

Pretend you can change into an animal for a day. Write several sentences about your day, using at least six of your spelling words. (Circle) each spelling word you used.

Activities for Spelling 10

Name _____   Week_____

1. _____   6. _____
2. _____   7. _____
3. _____   8. _____
4. _____   9. _____
5. _____   10. _____

Monday

Write each spelling word one time in pencil and then one time in pen or marker.

Tuesday

Write each spelling word. Look up each word in a dictionary and write the page number on which you found each word.

example: **again**—page 56   _____
                                              (title of your dictionary)

Wednesday

Draw a picture of a great big flower. Write each spelling word on one of the petals or on a leaf. Write a few sentences about flowers, using as many of your spelling words as you can. Circle the spelling words in your sentences.

Thursday

Write your spelling list in ABC order.

Activities for Spelling 11

Name _____ Week _____

1. _____   6. _____
2. _____   7. _____
3. _____   8. _____
4. _____   9. _____
5. _____   10. _____

Monday

Write each spelling word two times. Now give each spelling word a point value by adding two points for each vowel and three points for each consonant.

example: **beside**   **beside**   **3+2+3+2+3+2=15**

great   **great**   **3+3+2+2+3=13**

Tuesday

Write each spelling word. Look up each word in a dictionary and write any other word forms you find at the end of the entry.

example: **beside**   *besides*

great   *greater*   *greatest*   *greatly*

Wednesday

Pretend you are a clown. Write a letter to the circus asking for a job. Use at least six spelling words in your letter explaining why you are the best for the job. Underline your spelling words.

Thursday

Draw and color a picture of yourself dressed up in your clown suit and holding 10 balloons. Write your spelling words on the balloons in ABC order.

Activities for Spelling

Name _____   Week _____

1. _____   6. _____
2. _____   7. _____
3. _____   8. _____
4. _____   9. _____
5. _____   10. _____

Monday

Write each spelling word two times. Put a * next to your neatest writing of each spelling word.

Tuesday

Write each spelling word and then add "tag alongs," words that begin and end with the same letters as your spelling word. Connect them to your spelling words.

example:

```
                              b
                              a
                              l
         a   n   i   m   a   l
         n
         d
```

Wednesday

Pretend you work for a radio station. Write a commercial for your favorite snack food to convince other boys and girls to try your snack. Use at least six spelling words in your writing. Circle the spelling words.

Thursday

Write each spelling word. Write a rhyming word next to the spelling word.

example: **stair**   *chair*

             people   *steeple*

Activities for Spelling 13

Name _____   **Week** _____

1. _____   6. _____
2. _____   7. _____
3. _____   8. _____
4. _____   9. _____
5. _____   10. _____

Monday

Write each of the spelling words one time normally and then one time in letter boxes.

example: **letter**   l e t t e r

Tuesday

Pretend that you are vacationing on another planet. Write a letter back to a friend on Earth describing your adventures on this planet. Include your spelling words in your letter. Circle them.

Wednesday

Write each of your spelling words two or three times around to form circles of each spelling word.

example:

letter letter letter

Thursday

Write a sentence for each of the spelling words. Use a classmate's name in each of your sentences.

example: **I wrote a letter to *Michelle*.**

Activities for Spelling

Name _____   Week _____

1. _____   6. _____
2. _____   7. _____
3. _____   8. _____
4. _____   9. _____
5. _____   10. _____

Monday

Write each spelling word horizontally and vertically, sharing the same beginning letter. (Circle) that beginning letter.

example:

     (w) h e n
     h
     e
     n

Tuesday

Write each spelling word in a sentence using a contraction somewhere in the sentence.

example: **I *don't* know when the bell rings.**

Wednesday

Write each spelling in "word wagons" by writing the beginning and ending letters on each wheel and using the word as the wagon bed.

example:

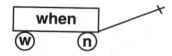

Thursday

Write a few long sentences using as many spelling words as you can in each one. Try to think of ways to use two or three spelling words in each sentence. Draw a box around each one you use.

Activities for Spelling 15

Name _____ Week _____

1. _____   6. _____
2. _____   7. _____
3. _____   8. _____
4. _____   9. _____
5. _____   10. _____

Monday

Write each spelling word. Write it again using one color for all the vowels and one color for all the consonants.

Tuesday

Dictate sentences to a parent or a friend for words 1–5. Have them write the sentences down for you. Then have them dictate a sentence to you for words 6–10. You write these down. Draw a | box | around each spelling word.

Wednesday

Write each spelling word in a "beginning letter blitz." Write each word over and over to form the shape of its beginning letter.

example:

```
>   e v e r y
r
e   e v e r y
>
e   e v e r y
```

Thursday

Write each spelling word and then write the dictionary page number on which you find each word.

example: **every**—page 74 _____

(title of your dictionary)

Activities for Spelling 16

Name _____   Week_____

1. _____   6. _____
2. _____   7. _____
3. _____   8. _____
4. _____   9. _____
5. _____   10. _____

Monday

Write each spelling word two times. Write each spelling word a third time drawing a box around each vowel.

example: **around**   **around**   a r o u n d

                above   **above**   a b o v e

Tuesday

Write each spelling word in a sentence that has a cartoon character or superhero's name as the subject. Underline each spelling word.

example: **Cinderella walked <u>around</u> the castle.**

                Superman flew <u>above</u> the building.

Wednesday

Write all the spelling words in ABC order. Skip lines so you will have space to go back and (circle) each consonant in the spelling words.

example: a ⓑ o ⓥ e   a ⓡ o u ⓝⓓ

Thursday

Write each spelling word in a question using a cartoon character or superhero as the subject.

example: **Did Cinderella run <u>around</u> in glass slippers?**

                Is that Superman flying <u>above</u> your house?

Activities for Spelling

Name _____   **Week** _____

1. _____	**6.** _____
2. _____	**7.** _____
3. _____	**8.** _____
4. _____	**9.** _____
5. _____	**10.** _____

Monday

Write each spelling word normally, then in all capital letters, and then one more time normally.

example: **forest   FOREST   forest**

Tuesday

Write each spelling word in "smiley faces" by using the beginning and ending letters as eyes and writing the complete word as the mouth.

example:

Wednesday

Write each spelling word. Look up each spelling word in a dictionary. Beside each spelling word, write the entry word that comes after your spelling word.

example: **forest**   *forestry*

Thursday

Write a paragraph of at least six sentences about a favorite animal. Include as many of your spelling words as you can. Draw a box around each spelling word you use.

Activities for Spelling 18

☞ You will need a WORD SEARCH page for Thursday.

Name _____   *Week* _____

1. _____   6. _____
2. _____   7. _____
3. _____   8. _____
4. _____   9. _____
5. _____   10. _____

Monday

Write each spelling word one time normally and then one time in "double doodle" by holding two pencils or a pen and a pencil together while writing.

example: **feather**

Tuesday

Write each spelling word two times and then think of a single word that begins and ends with the same letters as each of the spelling words.

example: **hungry**   **hungry**   *hairy*

                        afraid   **afraid**   *and*

Wednesday

Write words 1–5 in sentences. Write words 5–10 in questions. Don't forget to use correct punctuation.

Thursday

Use all your spelling words to make a word search. After filling it in, have a friend or family member circle the spelling words. Write down each word found in the word search.

Activities for Spelling 19

Name _____   Week _____

1. _____	6. _____
2. _____	7. _____
3. _____	8. _____
4. _____	9. _____
5. _____	10. _____

Monday

Write each spelling word. Write it again using the following code.

example: **word** = ⚠ ● ■ ÷

a = ✳	b = △	c = ↑	d = ÷	e = ☐	f = ↓	g = ▼	h = ⊙	i = ✕
j = ○	k = ▽	l = ☆	m = ♥	n = →	o = ●	p = ▫	q = ←	r = ■
s = ♡	t = ⊠	u = ▲	v = +	w = ⚠	x = ✿	y = ★	z = ⊗	

Tuesday

Write a sentence for each of your spelling words. Include a plural noun (a word that means more than one person, place, or thing) somewhere in your sentence.

example: **The kittens like to <u>brush</u> against my leg.**

Wednesday

Write each spelling word as a "word wagon," using the beginning and ending letters on each wheel and using the word as the wagon bed.

example:

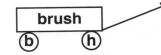

Thursday

Write each spelling word. Then look up each word in a dictionary and write the guide words from that page (the two words you find at the top of each page telling you the first and last word on that page).

example: **brush**   guide words = **bruise/Brussels**

Activities for Spelling **20**

Name _____ Week _____

1. _____   6. _____
2. _____   7. _____
3. _____   8. _____
4. _____   9. _____
5. _____   10. _____

Monday

Write each spelling word. Write it again capitalizing all the vowels. Write it one more time normally.

example: **said   sAId   said**

            afraid   AfrAId   afraid

Tuesday

Pretend you are away at camp. Write a letter home to Mom or Dad. Include all of the spelling words in your letter. Draw <u>two lines</u> under each spelling word.

Wednesday

Write your spelling words. Then write them in "telephone code" by writing a number value for each letter as it appears on the buttons of your telephone. Give letters Q and Z a value of 0.

example: **said   =   7-2-4-3**

1	ABC 2	DEF 3
GHI 4	JKL 5	MNO 6
PRS 7	TUV 8	WXY 9
*	OPER 0	#

Thursday

Use words 1 + 2 in a sentence, and continue with words 3 + 4, 5 + 6, 7 + 8, and 9 + 10 in sentences together. Underline the spelling words in each sentence.

example: **1+2. Mother <u>said</u> you were <u>afraid</u> of lightning.**

Activities for Spelling 21

Name _____ Week _____

1. _____   6. _____
2. _____   7. _____
3. _____   8. _____
4. _____   9. _____
5. _____   10. _____

Monday

Write each spelling word across and down using the same beginning letter.

example:

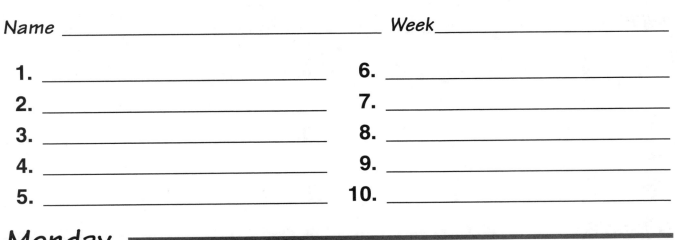

Tuesday

Write each spelling word by cutting out and pasting together letters from old newspapers and magazines.

Wednesday

Write each spelling word. Write another word that looks very similar to the spelling word. Write the spelling word again.

example: **giant**   *grant*   **giant**

Thursday

Write each spelling word in a sentence and include the name of a different month in each of your sentences.

Activities for Spelling 22

Name _____   Week_____

1. _____   6. _____
2. _____   7. _____
3. _____   8. _____
4. _____   9. _____
5. _____   10. _____

Monday

Write each spelling word one time in pencil and one time in pen. (Circle) your neatest writing of each word.

Tuesday

Make a "word train" out of your spelling list. Write each word on a train car and write its beginning letter and ending letter on one of the car's wheels.

example:

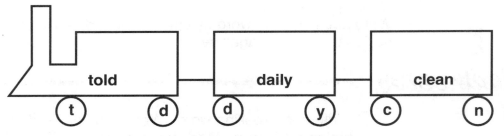

Wednesday

Write a "tongue twister" sentence for each spelling word by using as many words beginning with the same letter as your word as you can think of. Underline the beginning letters you are repeating. Circle each spelling word.

example: <u>T</u>ommy (<u>told</u>) <u>T</u>ed not <u>t</u>o <u>t</u>ickle <u>t</u>urtles.
                <u>D</u>an's <u>d</u>og <u>d</u>igs <u>d</u>irt (<u>daily</u>).

Thursday

Write your spelling list in ABC order. Have another person give you a practice test on your words.

Activities for Spelling

Name _____   **Week** _____

1. _____   6. _____
2. _____   7. _____
3. _____   8. _____
4. _____   9. _____
5. _____   10. _____

Monday

Write each spelling word two times. Try to make a new word by using as many of the letters in your spelling word as possible. You may rearrange the letters.

examples: **wagon   wagon   ago**   **star   star   rats**

Tuesday

Write each spelling word as a "smiley face," using the beginning and ending letters as eyes and the whole word as a mouth.

example:

Wednesday

Write each spelling word. Look up each word and copy the sentence from the dictionary in which each word is used. Remember to copy the sentence, not the definition!

example: **wagon**—Father used a wagon to carry wood into the shed.

star—The star shone brightly in the night sky.

Thursday

Make a chart with three columns—**Spelling Word**, **Same Beginning**, and **Same Ending**. Fill in your chart with each spelling word, a new word with the same beginning letter, and a new word with the same ending letter.

Spelling Word	Same Beginning	Same Ending
wagon	welcome	rain

Activities for Spelling 24

Name _____   *Week* _____

1. _____   6. _____
2. _____   7. _____
3. _____   8. _____
4. _____   9. _____
5. _____   10. _____

Monday

Write your spelling words two times. Write them one more time using capital letters for vowels and lowercase letters for consonants.

example: **nice**   **nice**   **nIcE**

Tuesday

Write your spelling words. Then write them in "telephone code" by looking on your telephone number buttons and giving each letter in your word a number value. Give letters Q and Z a value of 0. Write the word again.

example: **nice**   **6-4-2-3**   **nice**

Wednesday

Write your spelling words. Then look them up in your dictionary and write the page number on which you found each word.

example: **nice**—page 165 _____
(title of your dictionary)

Thursday

Write sentences using your spelling words this way:

1. words 1 and 2 in a statement
2. words 3 and 4 in a question
3. words 5 and 6 in a statement
4. words 7 and 8 in a question
5. words 9 and 10 in a statement

Activities for Spelling

Name _____   Week _____

1. _____   6. _____
2. _____   7. _____
3. _____   8. _____
4. _____   9. _____
5. _____   10. _____

Monday

Write each spelling word two times and then write another word that begins with the same letter. Underline the beginning letters.

example: **listen**   **listen**   **letter**

Tuesday

Write spelling words 1–5 in statements. Write spelling words 6–10 in questions. Draw a box around each spelling word.

Wednesday

"Star-write" each spelling word.

example:

Thursday

Write a letter to your favorite sports hero or musician. Include all your spelling words and underline each one in your letter.

Activities for Spelling 26

☞ You will need a WORD SEARCH page for Thursday.

Name _____   Week_____

1. _____   6. _____
2. _____   7. _____
3. _____   8. _____
4. _____   9. _____
5. _____   10. _____

Monday

Write each spelling word two times normally and one time in "spots."

example: **fish**   **fish**   f i s h

Tuesday

Write spelling words 1–5 across (horizontally) and down (vertically) sharing the same beginning letter. (Circle) the beginning letter.

example: ⓕ**ish**
               i
               s
               h

Wednesday

Write words 6–10. Then give each consonant a value of two and each vowel a value of three. Add the letter values together to get a total for each word. Write the word one more time.

example: **fish**   **2+3+2+2=9**   **fish**

Thursday

Make a word search with your spelling words. Try to hide each spelling word two times within your word search.

Activities for Spelling 27

Name _____ Week_____

1. _____   6. _____
2. _____   7. _____
3. _____   8. _____
4. _____   9. _____
5. _____   10. _____

Monday ──────────────────────────

Write each spelling word one time normally and then one time in "double doodle" by holding two pencils or a pen and a pencil together while writing.

example:

hungry

Tuesday ──────────────────────────

Write each spelling word and then think of two other words that can be made by using letters from your spelling word. Write them down next to your spelling word.

example: **hungry** *hung rug*   **leaves** *seal slave*

Wednesday ──────────────────────────

Write each spelling word and then a sentence with words that begin with each letter of your spelling word. Underline each letter as you use it.

example: **hungry—Mom helped us pick nine green roses yesterday.**

leaves—Let's eat all the vegetables except the spinach.

Thursday ──────────────────────────

Write each spelling word in "pea pods" by placing each letter of the word in the "peas" of the "pea pod." Group pods together that have the same number of letters or "peas."

Activities for Spelling

Name _____ Week_____

1. _____   6. _____
2. _____   7. _____
3. _____   8. _____
4. _____   9. _____
5. _____   10. _____

Monday

Write each spelling word in a word box by writing the word across the top, down the right side, across the bottom, and up the left side to close the box.

example:

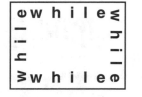

Tuesday

Write each spelling word and then its definition from the dictionary.

example: **while—a period of time**

Wednesday

Write each spelling word and then write it again in "telephone code." Look on your phone and give each letter the assigned number value from the push buttons. Give letters Q and Z the value of 0.

example: **while   9-4-4-5-3**

Thursday

Write each spelling word in a question. Underline the spelling words.

example: **What will you do <u>while</u> I'm at school?**

Activities for Spelling

Name _____ *Week* _____

1. _____   6. _____
2. _____   7. _____
3. _____   8. _____
4. _____   9. _____
5. _____   10. _____

Monday

Write each spelling word three times. (Circle) your neatest writing for each.

Tuesday

Cut out letters from old newspapers and magazines to spell words 1–5. Glue the words onto your paper. Use words 6–10 in a sentence. Underline each spelling word with a different colored crayon.

Wednesday

Use words 1–5 in a sentence. Draw a box around each word with a different colored crayon. Cut out letters from old newspapers and magazines to spell words 6–10. Glue the words onto your paper.

Thursday

Make a chart with three columns—**Spelling Word**, **Same Beginning**, and **Same Ending**. Fill in your chart with the spelling words, a new word with the same beginning letter, and a new word with the same ending letter.

example:

Spelling Word	Same Beginning	Same Ending
read	(r)ain	san (d)

Activities for Spelling

☛ You will need a WORD SEARCH page for Thursday.

Name _____ Week_____

1. _____   6. _____
2. _____   7. _____
3. _____   8. _____
4. _____   9. _____
5. _____   10. _____

Monday

Write each spelling word two times normally and one time in "spots."

example: **fish**   **fish**   fish

Tuesday

- Write spelling words 1–5 across (horizontally) and down (vertically), sharing the same beginning letter. Circle the beginning letter.

example: ⓕish
               i
               s
               h

- Write words 6–10. Then give each consonant a value of two and each vowel a value of three. Add the letter values to get a total value for each word. Write the words one more time.

example: **fish**   **2+3+2+2=9**   **fish**

Wednesday

- Write words 1–5, following Tuesday's directions for 6–10.
- Write words 6–10, following Tuesday's directions for 1–5.

Thursday

Make a word search with your spelling words. Try to hide each spelling word two times within your word search.

Activities for Spelling

Name _____   Week _____

1. _____   6. _____
2. _____   7. _____
3. _____   8. _____
4. _____   9. _____
5. _____   10. _____

Monday

Write each spelling word two times in pencil and one time in pen.

Tuesday

- Write spelling words 1–5 normally and then in the code symbols below:

example: **word** = △ ● ■ ÷

a = ✳	b = △	c = ↑	d = ÷	e = □	f = ↓	g = ▼	h = ⊙	i = ✕
j = ○	k = ▽	l = ☆	m = ♥	n = →	o = ●	p = ⊡	q = ←	r = ■
s = ♡	t = ⊠	u = ▲	v = +	w = △	x = ✿	y = ★	z = ⊗	

- Use spelling words 6–10 each in a separate question. Circle each spelling word with a different colored crayon.

Wednesday

- Use words 1–5 in separate questions. Draw a box around each spelling word with a different colored crayon.
- Write words 6–10 normally and then in code from the box above.

Thursday

Write each spelling word. Then look up each word in a dictionary and write the guide words from the page on which you found each spelling word. (Guide words are the first and last words on each dictionary page and are written in **boldface** type at the top of each dictionary page.)

example: **word** guide words = **wool/work**

Section Two

Level Two
Activities for
Spelling

Activities for Spelling 1

Name _____   Week _____

1. _____   7. _____

2. _____   8. _____

3. _____   9. _____

4. _____   10. _____

5. _____   11. _____

6. _____   12. _____

Monday

Write each spelling word under the correct guide words.

example:

abacus-cursive	**curtain-indigo**	**indirect-number**	**numeral-sarong**	**sash-Zulu**
bark	*elm*	*leaf*	*roots*	*tree*

Tuesday

Write your spelling words in alphabetical order, being sure to skip lines. Go back and insert a new word that would come between each spelling word in alphabetical order.

Wednesday

Write your choice of sentence (declarative, interrogative, imperative, or exclamatory) for each of the spelling words. Go back and circle all of the **articles** (a, an, the). Underline each spelling word.

example: The bark of a tree is very tough.

Thursday

Use a **Venn diagram** to organize your spelling words. Label it "**Two Vowels or More**" on the left, "**Two Consonants or More**" on the right, and "**At Least Two Vowels and Two Consonants**" in the middle.

Activities for Spelling 2

Name _____   Week _____

1. _____	7. _____
2. _____	8. _____
3. _____	9. _____
4. _____	10. _____
5. _____	11. _____
6. _____	12. _____

Monday

Write each spelling word. Write it again in cursive letters. Write it again normally.

example: **word**   *word*   **word**

Tuesday

• Write words 1–6 horizontally and vertically, sharing the same beginning letter. Circle the beginning letter.

example: (**w**) **ord**
        o
        r
        d

• Write words 7–12. Look them up in the dictionary and write the page number on which you found each word.

example: **word**—page 134 _____
                                    (title of your dictionary)

Wednesday

• Write words 1–6, using Tuesday's directions for 7–12.

• Write words 7–12, using Tuesday's directions for 1–6.

Thursday

Write a letter to your favorite storybook character, including as many spelling words as you can. Underline each spelling word in the letter.

Don't forget to use good letter form (*date, greeting, body, closing,* and *signature*).

Activities for Spelling 3

Name _____   Week_____

1. _____   7. _____
2. _____   8. _____
3. _____   9. _____
4. _____   10. _____
5. _____   11. _____
6. _____   12. _____

Monday

Write each spelling word two times and then write the encyclopedia volume number in which you would look to find information about each word. Use the volume number guide below.

A–C	D–F	G–I	J–L	M–O	P–R	S–U	V–X	Y–Z
1	2	3	4	5	6	7	8	9

example: **whale   whale   volume 8**

Tuesday

Write sentences for words 1–6 that use commas somewhere in each sentence.

example: **Dr. Gordon, a marine biologist, studies whales.**

Write spelling words 7–12 and then give each letter a value by using the numbers you used on Monday as volume numbers. Add the numbers to get a total value.

example: **wheel   8+3+2+2+4 = 19**

Wednesday

Write spelling words 1–6 and then give each letter a value and total using the volume number for each letter.

example: **whale   8+3+1+4+2 = 18**

Thursday

Write your spelling words in alphabetical order. **Be sure to skip lines**. Go back and insert a new word that would come between each of your spelling words in alphabetical order.

Activities for Spelling 4

Name _____ Week _____

1. _____   7. _____
2. _____   8. _____
3. _____   9. _____
4. _____   10. _____
5. _____   11. _____
6. _____   12. _____

Monday

Write each spelling word two times and then write a new word that has the same vowel sound. Circle the vowel in the new word.

example: **nice   nice   k(i)te**

Tuesday

• Write words 1–6 in "sailboat" style.

example:

• Look up words 7–12 in the dictionary. Write the entry word that comes before your spelling word, the spelling word itself, and then the entry word that comes after your spelling word.

example: **wool   word   wording**

Wednesday

• Look up words 1–6, following Tuesday's directions for 7–12.
• Write words 7–12 in "sailboat" style.

Thursday

• Dictate a sentence to an adult at home for each spelling word (1–6). Have the adult write each sentence on your paper.

• Have an adult dictate a sentence to you for each spelling word (7–12) and you write them down. Then ⟨circle⟩ each spelling word.

Activities for Spelling

☛ You will need a WORD SEARCH page for Thursday.

Name _____   *Week* _____

1. _____	7. _____
2. _____	8. _____
3. _____	9. _____
4. _____	10. _____
5. _____	11. _____
6. _____	12. _____

Monday

Write each spelling word and then use your dictionary to write down the page number on which you found each word.

Tuesday

Write each spelling word in "word spikes" by thinking of words that begin or end with each of the letters of the spelling word. Alternate the beginning and ending words with each new letter.

example:

```
        t       h
        a       i
    f r a i l
        r   s   o
        o   k   o
        m       p
```

Wednesday

Write sentences for each of your spelling words. Underline the subject of each sentence one time and the verb two times.

example: **The frail little <u>bird</u> <u>flew</u> away.**

Thursday

Create a word search with all your spelling words. Try to include words from last week's lesson as well.

Activities for Spelling

Name _____   Week _____

1. _____   7. _____
2. _____   8. _____
3. _____   9. _____
4. _____   10. _____
5. _____   11. _____
6. _____   12. _____

Monday

Make a chart and label it <u>One Vowel</u>, <u>Two Vowels</u>, <u>Three Vowels</u>, and <u>Four Vowels</u>. Fill in the chart by writing each spelling word under the correct heading.

example:

One Vowel	**Two Vowels**	**Three Vowels**	**Four Vowels**
draw	below	raise	opposite

Tuesday

Write each spelling word and then write it again in international Morse code using the guide below.

A	• —	F	• • — •	K	— • —	P	• — — •	U	• • —
B	— • • •	G	— — •	L	• — • •	Q	— — • —	V	• • • —
C	— • — •	H	• • • •	M	— —	R	• — •	W	• — —
D	— • •	I	• •	N	— •	S	• • •	X	— • • —
E	•	J	• — — —	O	— — —	T	—	Y	— • — —
								Z	— — • •

example: **d r a w** — • • • — • — •   **b e l o w** — • • • • • — • • — — — • — —

Wednesday

Write a sentence for each of your spelling words. Include a list in each sentence. Remember to use commas in your lists.

example: **Sam likes to draw horses, dogs, and sheep.**
Cheese, bacon, turkey, and ham make good sandwiches.

Thursday

Write each spelling word two times and then tell in which part of the dictionary it could be found.

Beginning	**Middle**	**End**
A–H	I–P	Q–Z

example: draw   draw   *beginning*

　　　　　　　　　　　　　　　　　　　　　Level Two Activities

Activities for Spelling 7

Name _____　Week _____

1. _____　　　7. _____
2. _____　　　8. _____
3. _____　　　9. _____
4. _____　　　10. _____
5. _____　　　11. _____
6. _____　　　12. _____

Monday

Write each spelling word and then use your dictionary to locate the words. Write the guide words from the top of the dictionary page on which you found each spelling word.

Tuesday

Write each spelling word in "beginning letter blitz" by writing your words over and over to form the shape of their beginning letters.

example:

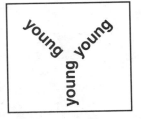

Wednesday

Write sentences for each of your spelling words. Draw a line dividing the subject (naming part) of each sentence from the predicate (telling part) of each sentence.

example: **The young squirrel / chased its tail.**

Thursday

Write each spelling word. Then make two other words by rearranging some of the letters from each word.

example: **young—gun**　　　**you**

Activities for Spelling

Name _____   Week_____

1. _____   7. _____
2. _____   8. _____
3. _____   9. _____
4. _____   10. _____
5. _____   11. _____
6. _____   12. _____

Monday

Write each spelling word one time in lowercase letters and then write it again in capital letters.

example: **pony   PONY**

Tuesday

Write your spelling words in "sailboat" style.

example:

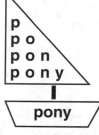

Wednesday

Have an adult at home dictate a sentence to you to write down for each spelling word in numbers 1–6. Write your own sentences for words 7–12. Draw a (circle) around each spelling word.

Thursday

Write all your spelling words in alphabetical order—first list them A through Z and then put them in reverse order from Z through A.

example: A—Z: **bell   card   even   four   math**

Z—A: **math   four   even   card   bell**

Activities for Spelling 9

Name _____ Week_____

1. _____   7. _____
2. _____   8. _____
3. _____   9. _____
4. _____   10. _____
5. _____   11. _____
6. _____   12. _____

Monday

Write each spelling word. Go back and <u>underline</u> each vowel. Then write each spelling word in a box according to how many vowels there are.

example:

Fewer Than Three	Exactly Three	More Than Three
shine	leave	earlier

Tuesday

Write each spelling word. Look up each word in a dictionary, write the page number, and then write the entry word that comes just before your spelling word in the dictionary.

example: **shine**—page 265   <u>**shin**</u>

   leave—page 127   <u>**leather**</u>

Wednesday

Write a command sentence for each spelling word.

example: **Shine your shoes before you wear them.**

   Do not leave the front door open.

Thursday

Write each spelling word three times correctly.

example: **shine   shine   shine**

   leave   leave   leave

Activities for Spelling **10**

☞ You will need a WORD SEARCH page for Thursday.

Name _____ Week_____

1. _____ 7. _____
2. _____ 8. _____
3. _____ 9. _____
4. _____ 10. _____
5. _____ 11. _____
6. _____ 12. _____

Monday

Write each spelling word. Then look up each word in a dictionary to find out its part-of-speech label (this tells you if the word is used as a noun, verb, adjective, adverb, etc.) A word may be used in more than one of these ways.

example: **rain—*noun, verb***

Tuesday

Write each spelling word and then make up a sentence by using words that begin with each letter of your spelling word. Underline each of the beginning letters as you use them.

example: **rain—<u>R</u>ebecca <u>a</u>wakened <u>i</u>n the <u>n</u>ight.**

Wednesday

Write each spelling word. Write it again in "telephone code" by assigning each letter a number from the number buttons on your telephone. Give "Q" and "Z" a value of 0.

example: **rain = 7-2-4-6**

```
 1    2ABC   3DEF
 4GHI 5JKL   6MNO
 7PRS 8TUV   9WXY
 *    0OPER  #
```

Thursday

Design a word search by using all of the spelling words. Add words from other spelling lists as well.

Activities for Spelling 11

Name _____   Week_____

1. _____   7. _____
2. _____   8. _____
3. _____   9. _____
4. _____   10. _____
5. _____   11. _____
6. _____   12. _____

Monday

Write each spelling word one time normally and one time in "double doodle" by holding two pencils or one pencil and one pen together as you write each spelling word.

example: **hungry**   **hungry** (double doodle)

Tuesday

Make a chart with three columns—**Spelling Word**, **Same Beginning**, and **Same Ending.** Fill in the chart with your spelling words, a new word with the same beginning letter, and a new word with the same ending letter.

example:

Spelling Word	Same Beginning	Same Ending
easy	⒠mblem	carr⒴
near	ⓝeedle	roa⒭

Wednesday

Use each of your spelling words in commands. Underline each of your spelling words.

example: **Be <u>easy</u> when you handle baby kittens.**
Don't get <u>near</u> a campfire.

Thursday

Write each spelling word and then assign it a point value by adding 5 points for each vowel and 10 points for each of the consonants.

example: **easy**   5+5+10+5 = 25
near   10+5+5+10 = 30

     #2312 Activities for Any Spelling Unit

Activities for Spelling

Name _____   Week _____

1. _____   7. _____
2. _____   8. _____
3. _____   9. _____
4. _____   10. _____
5. _____   11. _____
6. _____   12. _____

Monday

Write each word forward, backward, and then forward again.

example: **spelling**   *gnilleps*   **spelling**

Tuesday

- Write sentences in tongue-twister style for words 1–6.

  example: **Sam says seven spelling words a second.**

- Look up words 7–12 in the dictionary. Write the word and the guide words from that page.

  example: **spelling**   guide words—**species/spend**

Wednesday

- Write sentences in tongue-twister style for words 7–12.
- Look up words 1–6 in the dictionary. Write the word and its guide words from that page.

Thursday

- Have an adult in your home give you a practice spelling test on paper.
- Use each of your spelling words orally in a statement and a question and ask the adult to sign below.

_____
(signature)

Activities for Spelling 13

Name _____   Week _____

1. _____	7. _____
2. _____	8. _____
3. _____	9. _____
4. _____	10. _____
5. _____	11. _____
6. _____	12. _____

Monday

Write each spelling word in lowercase letters. Write it again in uppercase letters. Write it one more time in lowercase letters.

example: **word**   **WORD**   **word**

Tuesday

- Write words 1–6 normally and then in "telephone code." Give each letter of your spelling word a number value.

example: **word 9-6-7-3**

- Write words 7–12 in tongue-twister-style sentences. <u>Underline</u> the same beginning letters in your words.

example: **<u>W</u>ilma <u>w</u>ished <u>W</u>es lived <u>w</u>est of <u>W</u>ashington.**

Wednesday

- Write words 1–6 in tongue-twister sentences.
- Write words 7–12 once normally and again in "telephone code."

Thursday

Make a chart with three columns—**Spelling Word**, **Same Beginning**, and **Same Ending**. Fill in the chart with your spelling words, a new word with the same beginning letter, and a new word with the same ending letter.

Spelling Word	Same Beginning	Same Ending
word	(w)illow	car(d)

Activities for Spelling

Name _____ Week _____

1. _____	7. _____
2. _____	8. _____
3. _____	9. _____
4. _____	10. _____
5. _____	11. _____
6. _____	12. _____

Monday ━━━━━━━━━━━━━━━━━━━━━━━━━━━━━━━━━━

Write each spelling word three times.

Tuesday ━━━━━━━━━━━━━━━━━━━━━━━━━━━━━━━━━━

- Write spelling words 1–6. Look up each word in your dictionary. Write the phonetic spelling you found in the dictionary beside each word. Phonetic spelling is found in (parentheses) at the end of the entry and tells you how to pronounce the word.

example: **word** (*wurd*)

- Write each of the words 7–12 in a question.

Wednesday ━━━━━━━━━━━━━━━━━━━━━━━━━━━━━━━━━━

- Write each of the words 1–6 in a question.
- Look up words 7–12 in the dictionary.
- Write these words (7–12) and their phonetic spellings.

Thursday ━━━━━━━━━━━━━━━━━━━━━━━━━━━━━━━━━━

Write each spelling word correctly and then write it as a crossword.

example: **animal**
          a
          n
      animal
          m
          a
          l

Activities for Spelling

☞ You will need a WORD SEARCH page for Thursday.

Name _____   Week _____

1. _____   7. _____
2. _____   8. _____
3. _____   9. _____
4. _____   10. _____
5. _____   11. _____
6. _____   12. _____

Monday

Write each spelling word horizontally and vertically sharing the same beginning letter.

example: Ⓦ ord
          o
          r
          d

Tuesday

- Write spelling words 1–6 and then write each of them in code.

a = ✳	b = △	c = ↑	d = ÷	e = □	f = ↓	g = ▼	h = ⊙	i = ✕
j = ○	k = ▽	l = ☆	m = ♥	n = →	o = ●	p = ⊡	q = ←	r = ■
s = ♡	t = ⊠	u = ▲	v = +	w = ⬨	x = ✺	y = ★	z = ⊗	

- Use words 7–12 in questions. Highlight each spelling word with a yellow or orange marker.

Wednesday

- Use words 1–6 in a statement (a telling sentence) and highlight.
- Write words 7–12 and then write them again in code.

Thursday

Create a word search using all the spelling words.

Activities for Spelling

Name _____   Week _____

1. _____	7. _____
2. _____	8. _____
3. _____	9. _____
4. _____	10. _____
5. _____	11. _____
6. _____	12. _____

Monday

Write each spelling word in all capital letters, then in all lowercase letters, and then again in all capital letters.

example: **OTHER**   **other**   **OTHER**

Tuesday

• "Star-write" words 1–6.

• Write all your spelling words in alphabetical order (A–Z).

Wednesday

• Write all your spelling words in reverse alphabetical order (Z–A).

• "Star-write" words 7–12.

Thursday

• Have an adult at home give you a practice spelling test. After you spell each word on paper, tell the adult a sentence using that word.

• Turn your practice test in with the rest of your assignment and have an adult at home sign below letting me know you used good oral sentences.

_____

(signature)

Activities for Spelling 🔳17🔳

Name _____   Week_____

1. _____	**7.** _____
2. _____	**8.** _____
3. _____	**9.** _____
4. _____	**10.** _____
5. _____	**11.** _____
6. _____	**12.** _____

Monday

Write each spelling word two times. Then write each word again using capital letters for consonants and lowercase letters for vowels.

example: **spelling**   **spelling**   **SPeLLiNG**

Tuesday

- Cut out letters from old newspapers or magazines to spell words 1–6. Glue them onto your paper.

- Write sentences for words 7–12 using a pronoun in each sentence.

Wednesday

- Write sentences for spelling words 1–6 using a *contraction* in each.

- Cut out letters from old newspapers or magazines to spell the words 7–12. Glue them onto your paper.

Thursday

Write each spelling word and give a point value to each word by counting three points for each vowel and two points for each consonant.

Write the point value for each word beside it.

Circle the most valuable spelling word and draw a line under the spelling word with the least value. (If there is a tie, you may do more than one.)

example: (spelling)—18   <u>word</u>—9

other—12   **listen**—14

Activities for Spelling

Name _____   **Week** _____

1. _____   7. _____
2. _____   8. _____
3. _____   9. _____
4. _____   10. _____
5. _____   11. _____
6. _____   12. _____

Monday

Write each spelling word forward, backward, and then forward again.
example: **apple**   *elppa*   **apple**

Tuesday

• Write words 1–6 in "word spikes." Think of words that begin with each letter in your spelling word. Write the first word going down, the next word going up, and keep alternating them.

example:

```
          e              w
          i              o
    a     p      p       l      e
    p            i              a
    e            c              c
                 k              h
```

• Write all your spelling words in alphabetical order (A–Z).

Wednesday

• Write all your spelling words in reverse alphabetical order (Z–A).

• Write words 7–12 in "word spikes."

Thursday

Write six sentences combining your spelling words in this manner:
1. words 1 and 2 in a statement   5. words 9 and 10 in a question
2. words 3 and 4 in a question   6. words 11 and 12 in a
3. words 5 and 6 in a command   command
4. words 7 and 8 in a statement

Activities for Spelling

Name _____   Week _____

1. _____   7. _____
2. _____   8. _____
3. _____   9. _____
4. _____   10. _____
5. _____   11. _____
6. _____   12. _____

Monday

Write each spelling word two times normally. Then write each word using capital letters for consonants and lowercase letters for vowels.

example: **spelling**   **spelling**   **SPeLLiNG**

Tuesday

- Write sentences for words 1–6 in tongue-twister style. Underline the beginning letters in each word and circle each spelling word.

example: <u>S</u>ue <u>s</u>tudies ⟨<u>s</u>pelling⟩ on <u>S</u>unday <u>s</u>ometimes.

- Write words 7–12. Look each word up in the dictionary and write the guide words from the page (guide words are found in **boldface** type at the top of the dictionary page, telling you the first and last word on that page).

example: **spelling**   guide words—**spa/sport**

Wednesday

Do the same as for Tuesday, except write tongue-twister sentences for spelling words 7–12 and look up the guide words for words 1–6.

Thursday

Write each spelling word forward, backward, and then forward again.

example: **spelling**   *gnilleps*   **spelling**

Activities for Spelling

Name _____ Week _____

1. _____   7. _____
2. _____   8. _____
3. _____   9. _____
4. _____   10. _____
5. _____   11. _____
6. _____   12. _____

Monday

Write each spelling word two times. Then write a word next to the spelling word that begins with the same letter.

example: **word**   **word**   *weather*

Tuesday

• Find and cut out words 1–6 in the newspaper or cut out letters from the paper to spell each word and paste them onto your paper.

• Write each word (7–12) in a question. Draw a ☐box☐ around each spelling word.

Wednesday

• Find or spell words 7–12 from the newspaper.

• Write each word (1–6) in a statement. ⬭Circle⬭ each spelling word.

Thursday

Write each spelling word. Look each word up in the dictionary. Write the page number on which you found the word.

example: **word**—page 186 _____
                                    (title of your dictionary)

Activities for Spelling

Name _____   Week _____

1. _____   7. _____
2. _____   8. _____
3. _____   9. _____
4. _____   10. _____
5. _____   11. _____
6. _____   12. _____

Monday

Write each word two times. Then write each spelling word again, using capital letters for consonants and lowercase letters for vowels.

example: **spelling**   **spelling**   **SPeLLiNG**

Tuesday

• Write spelling words 1–6 horizontally and vertically, sharing the same beginning letter. Circle the beginning letter.

>   *example:* **Ⓢ pell**
>   **p**
>   **e**
>   **l**
>   **l**

• Cut out words or letters from a newspaper or a magazine to spell words 7–12.

Wednesday

• Cut out words or letters from a newspaper or a magazine to spell words 1–6.

• Write words 7–12 horizontally and vertically, sharing the same beginning letter.

Thursday

Write each odd-numbered word in a question and each even-numbered word in a statement.

Activities for Spelling 22

Name _____   Week _____

1. _____   7. _____
2. _____   8. _____
3. _____   9. _____
4. _____   10. _____
5. _____   11. _____
6. _____   12. _____

Monday

Write each spelling word and then tell how many vowels and consonants each spelling word has.

example:

Word	Vowels	Consonants
plenty	2	4
rainy	3	2

Tuesday

Write each spelling word in a sentence using all *plural nouns*.

example: **The *children* got *hugs* and *kisses* from their *parents*.**
We carry *umbrellas* on rainy *days*.

Wednesday

Make a chart with the guide words below. Write each spelling word under the correct guide words.

abacus–deal	**dear–inhale**	**initial–reunion**	**reveal–Zulu**
any	frosty	plenty	sunny

Thursday

Write each spelling word and then think of two new words you can spell from the letters in each spelling word.

example: **plenty—*yet, lent***

rainy—*any, air*

Activities for Spelling

Name _____   Week _____

1. _____   7. _____
2. _____   8. _____
3. _____   9. _____
4. _____   10. _____
5. _____   11. _____
6. _____   12. _____

Monday

Write each spelling word two times normally and then one more time in all capital letters.

example: **gentle   gentle   GENTLE**

Tuesday

Write each spelling word and then rearrange letters in the word to make two new words.

example: **gentle—*lent, eel***

Wednesday

Write a thank you letter to someone for a gift you received. Use at least eight of your spelling words. Draw a ⬚box⬚ around each of them in your letter.

Thursday

Write each spelling word in "word spikes" by thinking of words that begin and end with the letters of each spelling word. Alternate the beginning and ending words with each new letter.

example:

```
                    h
        e    l      a
        y    e      v
        g e n t l e
        a    e      a
        i    w      m
        t           e
```

Activities for Spelling

Name _____   Week_____

1. _____   7. _____
2. _____   8. _____
3. _____   9. _____
4. _____   10. _____
5. _____   11. _____
6. _____   12. _____

Monday

Write each word two times and then write a word that begins with the same sound.

example: **word**   **word**   ***weather***

Tuesday

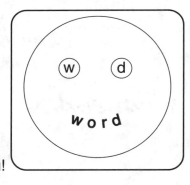

• Write words 1–6 in "smiley faces," using the beginning letter as the first eye and the ending letter as the second eye. Write the complete word as the smile.

example: **word**

• Write words 7–12 one time. Then dictate a sentence for each word to an adult at home and have him or her write it next to each word for you!

Wednesday

• Write words 1–6 one time. Then have an adult at home dictate a sentence to you for you to write next to each word.

• Write each word (7–12) in "smiley faces."

Thursday

Write a paragraph using all your spelling words. Try to stay on the same topic or tell a nice story in your paragraph. Be sure to reread it and check for spelling! Highlight each spelling word.

Activities for Spelling 25

Name _____ Week _____

1. _____   7. _____
2. _____   8. _____
3. _____   9. _____
4. _____   10. _____
5. _____   11. _____
6. _____   12. _____

Monday

Write each spelling word once normally. Write each word again, using a pencil for all consonants and a pen for each vowel. Write each one again normally.

Tuesday

• "Star-write" each of words 1–6.

example:

• Write words 7–12 in a sentence that also has a pronoun as the subject (the naming part).

example: **<u>They</u> spell very well.**

Wednesday

• Write words 1–6 in a sentence that also has a pronoun as the subject.

• "Star-write" words 7–12.

Thursday

• Write a paragraph including as many spelling words as you can. Go back and draw a box around each spelling word.

• Have an adult in your home drill you out loud on your spelling words.

Activities for Spelling 26

Name _____   Week _____

1. _____   7. _____
2. _____   8. _____
3. _____   9. _____
4. _____   10. _____
5. _____   11. _____
6. _____   12. _____

Monday

Write each spelling word two times and then in international Morse code.

example: sign sign ● ● ● / ● ● / — — — ● / — ●

A ● —	F ● ● — ●	K — ● —	P ● — — ●	U ● ● —
B — ● ● ●	G — — ●	L ● — ● ●	Q — — ● —	V ● ● ● —
C — ● — ●	H ● ● ● ●	M — —	R ● — ●	W ● — —
D — ● ●	I ● ●	N — ●	S ● ● ●	X — ● ● —
E ●	J ● — — —	O — — —	T —	Y — ● — —
				Z — — ● ●

Tuesday

- Write spelling words 1–6 in exclamatory sentences.

example: **What a beautiful sign you have painted!**

- Write spelling words 7–12 in sentences that include a comma of address.

example: **Rachel, did you hang up your clothes?**

Wednesday

- Write words 1–6 in sentences that include a comma of address.

example: **Children, don't forget to sign your letters.**

- Write spelling words 7–12 in exclamatory sentences.

example: **I told you to hang up your clothes!**

Thursday

Write a short descriptive paragraph, using at least eight spelling words. Go back and circle all of the articles (*a, an,* and *the*).

Activities for Spelling

Name _____   Week_____

1. _____   7. _____
2. _____   8. _____
3. _____   9. _____
4. _____   10. _____
5. _____   11. _____
6. _____   12. _____

Monday ▬▬▬▬▬▬▬▬▬▬▬▬▬▬▬▬▬▬▬▬▬▬▬▬▬▬▬

Write each spelling word two times in pencil and two times in red pen. No mistakes!

Tuesday ▬▬▬▬▬▬▬▬▬▬▬▬▬▬▬▬▬▬▬▬▬▬▬▬▬▬

• Locate words 1–6 in the dictionary. Write and <u>underline</u> the spelling word. In front of each spelling word, write the entry word that comes before the spelling word on the dictionary page and after the spelling word write the entry word that comes after the spelling word.

   example: **lake**   <u>**lamb**</u>   **lame**

• Write each of words 7–12 in a command sentence.

Wednesday ▬▬▬▬▬▬▬▬▬▬▬▬▬▬▬▬▬▬▬▬▬▬▬

• Write words 1–6 in command sentences.

• Look up words 7–12 in the dictionary. Write and <u>underline</u> the spelling word and then write the entry words that come before and after each spelling word on that dictionary page.

Thursday ▬▬▬▬▬▬▬▬▬▬▬▬▬▬▬▬▬▬▬▬▬▬▬▬▬

Write each spelling word once normally. Write each word a second time, using a pencil for the consonants and a red pen for each vowel. Write each spelling word one more time normally.

Activities for Spelling

Name _____   Week _____

1. _____   7. _____
2. _____   8. _____
3. _____   9. _____
4. _____   10. _____
5. _____   11. _____
6. _____   12. _____

Monday

Write each spelling word under the correct guide words.

example:

abacus-cursive   **curtain-indigo**   **indirect-rank**   **ransom-Zulu**
clue   flute   mute   suit

Tuesday

• Write spelling words 1–6 in sentences stating facts.

example: **Clue is the name of a board game.**

• Write spelling words 7–12 in sentences stating opinions.

example: **I think the flute is the best instrument.**

Wednesday

• Write spelling words 1–6 in sentences stating opinions.

example: **Teddy gave the best clue to the answer.**

Write spelling words 7–12 in sentences stating facts.

example: **The flute is a wind instrument.**

Thursday

Use a Venn diagram to organize your spelling words under these labels: **Fewer Than Three Vowels** (for the left section), **More Than Three Vowels,** (for the right section), and **Exactly Three Vowels** (for the center section).

Activities for Spelling

Name _____   Week _____

1. _____   7. _____
2. _____   8. _____
3. _____   9. _____
4. _____   10. _____
5. _____   11. _____
6. _____   12. _____

Monday

Use a Venn diagram to organize your spelling words. Label your diagram **Two or More Vowels** on the left side, **Two or More Consonants** on the right, and **Two or More Vowels and Consonants** in the middle.

Tuesday

Write each spelling word two times and then write the encyclopedia volume number in which you would look to find information on each word. Use the volume number guide below.

A–C	D–F	G–I	J–L	M–O	P–R	S–U	V–X	Y–Z
1	2	3	4	5	6	7	8	9

example: **giraffe**   **giraffe**—volume 3

Wednesday

Write sentences for words 1–6, using compound subjects.

example: **The giraffe and camel are new to the zoo.**

Write sentences for words 7–12, using compound predicates.

example: **My father cleaned the garage and mowed the lawn.**

Thursday

Write sentences for words 1–6, using compound predicates.

Write sentences for words 7–12, using compound subjects.

Activities for Spelling

Name _____ Week _____

1. _____		7. _____	
2. _____		8. _____	
3. _____		9. _____	
4. _____		10. _____	
5. _____		11. _____	
6. _____		12. _____	

Monday

Write each spelling word two times in a normal way. Then write it a third time using lowercase letters for consonants and uppercase for the vowels.

example: **word**   **word**   **wOrd**
             boat   **boat**   **bOAt**

Tuesday

• Write words 1–6 in a sentence.

• Write words 7–12 in a normal way and then write them in code.

example: **word** △ ● ■ ÷

a = ✳	b = △	c = ↑	d = ÷	e = ☐	f = ↓	g = ▼	h = ⊙	i = ✕
j = ◯	k = ▽	l = ☆	m = ♥	n = →	o = ●	p = ⊡	q = ←	r = ■
s = ♡	t = ⊠	u = ▲	v = +	w = △	x = ❀	y = ★	z = ⊗	

Wednesday

Do the same activities for Tuesday except write words 1–6 normally and then in code and write words 7–12 in sentences.

Thursday

Write all spelling words in alphabetical order. Have an adult at home give you a practice spelling test. Have that person sign below after the test.

_____
(signature)

Activities for Spelling

Name _____   Week_____

1. _____   7. _____
2. _____   8. _____
3. _____   9. _____
4. _____   10. _____
5. _____   11. _____
6. _____   12. _____

Monday

Print your spelling word one time and then write it in cursive letters.

example: **pony**   *pony*

Tuesday

- Write spelling words 1–6 in "sailboat" style.

example:

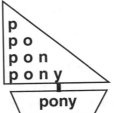

- Dictate a sentence to an adult at home for each of words 7–12 and have the adult write it on your paper. Go back and ⟨circle⟩ each spelling word.

Wednesday

- Have an adult at home dictate a sentence to you to write down for each of spelling words 1–6. Put a |box| around each spelling word.
- Write "sailboat" style for words 7–12.

Thursday

Write all your spelling words in alphabetical order—first A through Z and then in reverse order from Z through A.

example: A—Z: **bell   card   even   four   math**

     Z—A: **math   four   even   card   bell**

Activities for Spelling

Name _____   Week_____

1. _____   7. _____
2. _____   8. _____
3. _____   9. _____
4. _____   10. _____
5. _____   11. _____
6. _____   12. _____

Monday

Chart your spelling words by writing them under the correct headings: **One Vowel, Two Vowels, Three Vowels,** and **Four or More Vowels.**

Tuesday

• Write sentences for spelling words 1–6. Underline the complete subjects with <u>one line</u>. Underline the complete predicates with <u>two lines</u>.

example: **<u>The little yellow bird</u> <u>bathed in our birdbath.</u>**

• Write sentences for spelling words 7–12 using a compound predicate.

example: **I like to draw and color cartoons.**

Wednesday

• Write sentences for words 1–6 using a compound predicate.

• Write sentences for words 7–12. Underline the complete subject with one line and the complete predicate with two lines.

Thursday

Write each spelling word and then use your dictionary to find the entry word that comes after your spelling word in the dictionary.

Activities for Spelling 33

Name _____   Week _____

1. _____   7. _____

2. _____   8. _____

3. _____   9. _____

4. _____   10. _____

5. _____   11. _____

6. _____   12. _____

Monday

Write each spelling word two times and then write a word that both begins and ends with the same letters as the spelling word. Underline the beginning and ending letters on the new word.

example: **pencil   pencil   <u>p</u>ear<u>l</u>**

Tuesday

Write each spelling word "sailboat spelling" style. The sail is made by adding on letters one at a time, and the boat is made from a completed word.

example:

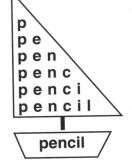

Wednesday

Write a paragraph about your favorite holiday. Include all your spelling words. Circle them in your paragraph.

Thursday

Write each spelling word. Write them again in "double doodle" style by holding two pencils or a pen and pencil at the same time as you write the word.

Activities for Spelling 34

Name _____   Week _____

1. _____   7. _____

2. _____   8. _____

3. _____   9. _____

4. _____   10. _____

5. _____   11. _____

6. _____   12. _____

Monday

Write each spelling word two times. Look up each word in the dictionary and write the entry word that comes before each spelling word.

Tuesday

Use a Venn diagram to organize your spelling words with these labels: **Fewer Than Three Vowels** (for the left section), **More Than Three Vowels** (for the right section), and **Exactly Three Vowels** (for the center section).

Wednesday

• Write interrogative sentences for words 1–6.

example: **Did you listen carefully to the lesson?**

• Write exclamatory sentences for words 7–12.

example: **Stop, do not blow that whistle!**

Thursday

• Write exclamatory sentences for words 1–6.

example: **Listen very carefully!**

• Write interrogative sentences for words 7–12.

example: **Is that you blowing that whistle?**

Activities for Spelling

☞ You will need a WORD SEARCH page for Thursday.

Name _____ Week _____

1. _____   7. _____
2. _____   8. _____
3. _____   9. _____
4. _____   10. _____
5. _____   11. _____
6. _____   12. _____

Monday

Write each spelling word normally, and then again as a crossword.

example: **happy**

h
a
happy
p
y

Tuesday

- Look up words 1–6 in the dictionary. Write the sentence in which the word is used (be sure it is the sentence and not the definition). <u>Underline</u> the spelling word.

- Write all of the spelling words in alphabetical order (A–Z).

Wednesday

- Look up words 7–12 in the dictionary. Write the sentence and <u>underline</u> the word.

- Write all of the spelling words in reverse alphabetical order (Z–A).

Thursday

- Make a word search with your new spelling words. Study for your spelling test.

- Have an adult in your home drill you on your words and sign below.

_____
(signature)

Activities for Spelling

👉 You will need a WORD SEARCH page for Thursday.

Name _____ *Week* _____

1. _____ 7. _____
2. _____ 8. _____
3. _____ 9. _____
4. _____ 10. _____
5. _____ 11. _____
6. _____ 12. _____

Monday

Write each spelling word horizontally and vertically, sharing the same beginning letter.

example: Ⓦ **ord**
　　　　　o
　　　　　r
　　　　　d

Tuesday

• Write spelling words 1–6 and then write each of them in code.

a = ✳	b = △	c = ↑	d = ÷	e = ☐	f = ↓	g = ▼	h = ⊙	i = ✕
j = ○	k = ▽	l = ☆	m = ♥	n = →	o = ●	p = ⊡	q = ←	r = ■
s = ♡	t = ⊠	u = ▲	v = +	w = ◬	x = ❋	y = ★	z = ⊗	

• Use each of words 7–12 in a question. Highlight each spelling word with a yellow or orange marker.

Wednesday

• Use each of words 1–6 in a statement and highlight.
• Write words 7–12 and then write them again in code.

Thursday

Create a word search using all of the spelling words.

Activities for Spelling 37

Name _____ Week _____

1. _____	7. _____
2. _____	8. _____
3. _____	9. _____
4. _____	10. _____
5. _____	11. _____
6. _____	12. _____

Monday

Print each spelling word, write it in script, and then print it one more time.

example: **camera**   *camera*   **camera**

Tuesday

Write your spelling words in alphabetical order and then write each spelling word under the correct guide words.

example: **camera**   **film**   **movie**   **print**   **slides**

abacus–cursive   **curtain–indigo**   **indirect–number**   **numeral–sarong**
camera   film   movie   prints

sash–Zulu
slides

Wednesday

- Write sentences that state an opinion for words 1–6.
example: **My camera is better than yours.**
- Write sentences that state a fact for words 7–12.
example: **Slides are shown by a slide projector.**

Thursday

- Write sentences for words 1–6 that state a fact.
- Write sentences for words 7–12 that state an opinion.

Activities for Spelling

Name _____   Week _____

1. _____	7. _____
2. _____	8. _____
3. _____	9. _____
4. _____	10. _____
5. _____	11. _____
6. _____	12. _____

Monday ─────────────────────────

Write each spelling word two times and then think of a new word that begins and ends with the same letters as the spelling word. Underline the beginning and ending letters.

example: **sudden**   **sudden**   **<u>sun</u>**

Tuesday ─────────────────────────

Write each spelling word and then look it up in your dictionary to find other forms of the word listed in the entry.

example: **sudden**   **<u>suddenly</u>**   **<u>suddenness</u>**

Wednesday ─────────────────────────

Write sentences for words 1–6 and include a pronoun in the subject of each sentence.

example: **<u>She</u> came to a sudden stop on the freeway.**

Write sentences for words 7–12 and include a pronoun in the predicate of each sentence.

example: **That is too much pepper for <u>her</u>.**

Thursday ─────────────────────────

For each spelling word write a sentence that contains a possessive pronoun. Circle the possessive pronoun.

example: **(Her) kitten meowed all of a sudden.**

Activities for Spelling

Name _____   Week_____

1. _____   7. _____
2. _____   8. _____
3. _____   9. _____
4. _____   10. _____
5. _____   11. _____
6. _____   12. _____

Monday

Write each spelling word two times. Then write a word that ends with the same letter. <u>Underline</u> each ending letter.

example: **car<u>d</u>**   **car<u>d</u>**   **ba<u>d</u>**

Tuesday

Write each word. Then look up each word in the dictionary and write the guide words you found on that page. (Guide words are found in **boldface** type at the top of each dictionary page, telling you the first and last words on that page.)

example: **card**   guide words = **camera/cat**

Wednesday

- Write your spelling words in alphabetical order (A–Z).
- Use words 1–6 in tongue-twister-style sentences.

example: **Can Carl carry Carol's card?**

Thursday

- Write your spelling words in reverse alphabetical order (Z–A).
- Use words 7–12 in tongue-twister-style sentences.

Activities for Spelling 40

Name _____ Week _____

1. _____ 7. _____
2. _____ 8. _____
3. _____ 9. _____
4. _____ 10. _____
5. _____ 11. _____
6. _____ 12. _____

Monday

Write each spelling word and then think of two words that can be made from letters in each spelling word.

example: **friendly** <u>**fried**</u> <u>**dine**</u>

Tuesday

Write each spelling word under the heading according to the number of vowels.
example:

One Vowel	Two Vowels	Three Vowels	Four or More Vowels
sing	tied	friendly	guidance

Wednesday

- For words 1–6 write sentences that have compound predicates.

example: **Sally <u>wrote</u> and <u>mailed</u> a friendly letter.**

- For words 7–12 write sentences that have compound subjects.

example: **<u>Bobby</u> and <u>Ted</u> tied a tail onto the kite.**

Thursday

Write sentences for your spelling words that have commas of address. You may use more than one spelling word in a sentence.

example: **Jason, do you think Mr. Smith's guidance was friendly and helpful?**

Activities for Spelling 41

Name _____   Week _____

1. _____   7. _____
2. _____   8. _____
3. _____   9. _____
4. _____   10. _____
5. _____   11. _____
6. _____   12. _____

Monday

Write each spelling word two times in print and two times in cursive style.

Tuesday

• Write words 1–6 in "word spikes."

```
example:     l                e
             o                k
             o                i
         s   p    e   l    l
         u        x           i
         n        i           m
                  t           e
```

• For each word (7–12), write a sentence using a compound word.

Wednesday

• For each word (1–6), write a sentence using a proper noun.
• Write spelling words 7–12 in "word spikes."

Thursday

• Write each spelling word and give a point value to each word by counting three points for each vowel and four points for each consonant. Write the point value for each word beside it.
• Circle the most valuable spelling word and draw a line under the spelling word with the least value. (If there is a tie, you may do more than one.)

example: hope—14   (sport) —19
             spoon—18   trap—15

Activities for Spelling 42

Name _____ Week _____

1. _____	7. _____
2. _____	8. _____
3. _____	9. _____
4. _____	10. _____
5. _____	11. _____
6. _____	12. _____

Monday

Print your spelling word, write it in cursive form, and then print it again.

example: **word**   *word*   **word**

Tuesday

- Write your own sentences using words 1–6. Use your spelling word in the subject (naming part) of the sentence. <u>Underline</u> the spelling word.

- Look up words 7–12 in the dictionary. Write the sentence from the entry and the page number.

  example: **The <u>word</u> is too hard to spell.** (page 174)

Wednesday

- Write your own sentences using spelling words 7–12 in the predicate (telling part) of each sentence.

- Look up words 1–6 in the dictionary. Write the sentence given and the page number.

  example: **Can you spell this <u>word</u> correctly?** (page 174)

Thursday

Write each spelling word four times. Have an adult in your home give you a practice spelling test.

Activities for Spelling

Name _____   Week _____

1. _____   7. _____
2. _____   8. _____
3. _____   9. _____
4. _____   10. _____
5. _____   11. _____
6. _____   12. _____

Monday

Print each spelling word twice. Then write it twice in cursive form.

Tuesday

- Look up words 1–6 in the dictionary. Write each word and its meaning.

example: **finch—a small songbird**

- Write words 7–12 normally. Write them again in letter boxes. Write them one more time normally.

example: **finch** f i n c h   **finch**

Wednesday

- Write words 1–6 normally, then in letter boxes, and again normally.
- Write words 7–12 and then their meanings from the dictionary.

Thursday

- Write your spelling words in alphabetical order.
- Have an adult in your home give you a practice test. Turn it in with your other spelling assignments. Write any misspelled words five times.

Section Three

Activities for Specific Skills

Vowel Sounds

Name _____ Week_____

(**Teacher Note:** *See pages 119–122 for appropriate words.*)

1. _____   7. _____
2. _____   8. _____
3. _____   9. _____
4. _____   10. _____
5. _____   11. _____
6. _____   12. _____

Monday

Write each spelling word two times in pencil and two times in pen. Any word that is misspelled must be written five times.

Tuesday

Write each spelling word. Then look it up in the dictionary and write its phonetic spelling (the way it is spelled to help you pronounce it).

example: **daily (dā´lē)**

Wednesday

- Write words 1–6. Then have an adult in your home dictate a sentence to you to write for each word. Draw a box around the spelling word in the sentence. An adult in your home can help you check your spelling.
- Write words 7–12 twice and then for each word write another that has the same vowel sound as the spelling word.

Thursday

- Write words 7–12. Then, for each spelling word dictate a sentence to an adult in your home. Have that person write the sentence down for you!
- Write words 1–6 twice and then write a word that has the same vowel sound.

Two Vowels Go Walking!

Name _____ **Week** _____

> **Rule:** When two vowels are together, the first one usually has a long vowel sound. "When two vowels go walking, the first one does the talking!"

(**Teacher Note:** *See page 123 for appropriate words.*)

1. _____   **7.** _____

2. _____   **8.** _____

3. _____   **9.** _____

4. _____   **10.** _____

5. _____   **11.** _____

6. _____   **12.** _____

Monday

Write each spelling word once normally. Write it again, underlining the two vowels and then a third time, circling the long vowel.

example: **chain   ch<u>ai</u>n   ch⊙in**

Tuesday

• Write words 1–6 in "smiley faces," placing the two vowels in the eyes and then writing the complete word for the mouth.

example: **chain**

• Write a sentence using spelling words 7–12 with as many other words with the same vowel sound as you can. Underline each spelling word.

example: **Ray made a paper <u>chain</u> for Jane.**

Wednesday

• Write sentences using words 1–6 in the same way as Tuesday's lesson.

• Write words 7–12 in "smiley faces."

Thursday

Write each spelling word. Beside each word write the first vowel + second vowel = the long vowel sound. Write each word again in all capital letters.

example: **chain   a + i = long a   CHAIN**

Vowel-Consonant-Silent "E"

Name _____ Week_____

Rule: Words spelled with a vowel-consonant-silent "e" pattern have a long vowel sound.

(**Teacher Note:** *See page 123 for appropriate words.*)

1. _____   7. _____
2. _____   8. _____
3. _____   9. _____
4. _____   10. _____
5. _____   11. _____
6. _____   12. _____

Monday

Write each spelling word once in lowercase letters, again in all uppercase letters, and then again in lowercase letters.

example: **lake   LAKE   lake**

Tuesday

- Write words 1–6 and then use your dictionary to find and copy the phonetic spelling for each. (The phonetic spelling is found after the entry and tells you how to pronounce the word.)

example: **lake   (lāk)**

- Use spelling words 7–12 in a question. Then answer the question, restating much of it.

example: **Did you swim in the lake?   Yes, I did swim in the lake.**

Wednesday

- Use spelling words 1–6 in a question and then answer each question, restating much of it.
- Write words 7–12 and then use your dictionary to find and copy the phonetic spelling of each.

Thursday

- Write your spelling words in alphabetical order from A–Z.
- Have an adult at home give you a practice spelling test. Write any misspelled words five times.

"R"-Controlled Words

Name _____ *Week* _____

> **Rule:** Many words have vowels that do not have a short or long sound because they are followed by the letter "r." You will hear the "r" very clearly controlling the vowel sound.

(**Teacher Note:** *See page 124 for appropriate words.*)

1. _____   7. _____
2. _____   8. _____
3. _____   9. _____
4. _____   10. _____
5. _____   11. _____
6. _____   12. _____

Monday

Write each spelling word one time. Write it again, noting the "r" controlled sound by circling the vowel and following "r."

example: **born   b (or) n**

Tuesday

- Write words 1–6 in a statement.
- Write words 7–12 in a question.

Wednesday

- Write all your spelling words. Then look them up in your dictionary and copy down the special pronunciation spelling at the end of the entry.

example: **born   (bôrn)**

Thursday

- Write spelling words 1–6 in questions using correct dialogue form. Include the speaker, commas, quotation marks, and question marks.

example: **Stan asked, "In what year were you born?"**

- Write spelling words 7–12 in statements using correct dialogue form. Include the speaker, commas, quotation marks, and periods.

example: **"The store is now closing," said the manager.**

"Y" Within Words

☞ You will need a WORD SEARCH page for Thursday.

Name _____   Week _____

> **Rule:** The letter "y" within a word usually makes the long "i" sound.

(Teacher Note: *See page 125 for appropriate words.)*

1. _____   7. _____

2. _____   8. _____

3. _____   9. _____

4. _____   10. _____

5. _____   11. _____

6. _____   12. _____

Monday

Write each spelling word two times normally and then write it by capitalizing the "y" within.

example: **cycle cycle cYcle**

Tuesday

• Write spelling words 1–6 one time normally and then one time in "telephone code" by assigning the number values of each letter from your telephone buttons. Give letters Q and Z a value of zero.

example: **cycle   2-9-2-5-3**

• Write sentences for words 7–12 in the past tense.

example: **A cyclone hit the island during the night.**

Wednesday

• Write sentences for words 1–6 in the future tense.

example: **The washer will run the spin cycle next.**

• Write spelling words 7–12 in "telephone code."

Thursday

Design a word search with all your spelling words. Use past spelling words to help fill your word search page.

"EI" Words

Name _____ **Week** _____

> **Rule:** The vowels "ei" come together in many words, especially after the letter "c." The letters "ei" often make the long "a" sound but can make other sounds too.

(**Teacher Note:** *See page 125 for appropriate words.*)

1. _____   7. _____
2. _____   8. _____
3. _____   9. _____
4. _____   10. _____
5. _____   11. _____
6. _____   12. _____

Monday

Write each spelling word across and down by sharing the same "e" from the vowel combination "ei."

example:
```
        t
        h
    t h e i r
        i
        r
```

Tuesday

- Write spelling words 1–6 one time normally and then one time drawing a box around the letters "ei."

example: **their th⬚ei⬚r**

- Write three different sentences by using words 7 and 8 together in the first sentence, 9 and 10 in the second, and 11 and 12 together in the third sentence.

Wednesday

- Write three sentences by using words 1 and 2 together in the first sentence, 3 and 4 in the second, and 5 and 6 together in the third.

- Write words 7–12 one time normally and then one time drawing a circle around the letters "ei."

example: **reign r(ei)gn**

Thursday

Write your spelling words in alphabetical order.

"IE" Words

Name _____ Week_____

> **Rule:** The vowels "ie" come together in many words. The letters "ie" often make the long "e" sound.

(**Teacher Note:** *See page 125 for appropriate words.*)

1. _____
2. _____
3. _____
4. _____
5. _____
6. _____
7. _____
8. _____
9. _____
10. _____
11. _____
12. _____

Monday

Write each spelling word normally two times and then one time with the "ie" written in capital letters.

example: **chief   chief   chIEf**

Tuesday

Write each spelling word under the guide words given below.

example:

abacus-cursive   **curtain-indigo**   **indirect-number**   **numeral-sarong**

believe   grief   mischief   pier

sash-Zulu

tier

Wednesday

Write each spelling word. Use your dictionary to write the phonetic spelling of each word.

example: **chief (chēf)**

Thursday

Pretend you are a private detective investigating the robbery of a very special museum exhibit of valuable jewelry. Use at least 10 of your "ie" spelling words in the paragraph. Underline each "ie" word in your writing.

Dropping the Silent "E"

Name _____ Week_____

> **Rule:** When a word ends with a vowel, a consonant, and a silent "e," you usually drop the silent "e" before adding "ed" or "ing."

(Teacher Note: *See page 126 for appropriate words.)*

1. _____
2. _____
3. _____
4. _____
5. _____
6. _____

7. _____
8. _____
9. _____
10. _____
11. _____
12. _____

Monday

Write the base word, write it again dropping the "e" and adding "ed," and then write it again dropping the "e" and adding "ing."

example: **paste**   *pasted*   *pasting*

Tuesday

- Write a sentence using the base word for words 1–6. Write a sentence using the "ed" past tense of words 7–12.
- Write all words 1–12 in the "ing" form (just words—sentences are not needed).

Wednesday

- Write a sentence using the "ed" past tense for each of words 1–6.
- Write a sentence using the base word for each of words 7–12. Write all base words and draw a red slash through the silent e.

Thursday

Look up all the base words in the dictionary. Write all forms of the words listed at the end of the entry and note the page number.

example: **paste**   *pastes*   *pasted*   *pasting*   (page 457)

Doubling the Last Consonant

Name _____   Week _____

> **Rule:** When a verb ends with a short vowel and one consonant, you usually double the last consonant before adding "ed" or "ing."

(**Teacher Note:** *See page 126 for appropriate words.*)

1. _____   7. _____
2. _____   8. _____
3. _____   9. _____
4. _____   10. _____
5. _____   11. _____
6. _____   12. _____

Monday

Write the spelling words. Write them again with the "ed" and "ing" endings.
example: **step**   *stepped*   *stepping*

Tuesday

- Write words 1–6 in sentences, first in the base word form and then again in the "ed" form.

  example: **Don't <u>step</u> on my toe. She <u>stepped</u> on my toe!**

- Write words 7–12 in all forms and circle the double consonants.

  example: **bat   ba(tt)ed   ba(tt)ing**

Wednesday

- Write words 7–12 in sentences, first in the base word form and then again in the "ing" form.

  example: **I am up to <u>bat</u> next. Rodney will be <u>batting</u> next.**

- Write words 1–6 in all forms and circle the double consonants.

  example: **step   ste (pp) ed   ste (pp) ing**

Thursday

Write each form of all words again. Write only the double consonants in red pen (all other letters are in pencil).

Words Ending in "Y"

Name _____   Week _____

> **Rule:** When a word ends in a consonant followed by the letter "y," you will change the "y" to "i" before adding an ending. Do not change the "y" to "i" when you add the ending "ing."

(**Teacher Note:** *See page 126 for appropriate words.*)

1. _____   7. _____
2. _____   8. _____
3. _____   9. _____
4. _____   10. _____
5. _____   11. _____
6. _____   12. _____

Monday

Write each form of your spelling words under these headings:

Base Word	**"ing" Form**	**"ed" Form**
hurry	hurrying	hurried

Tuesday

• Use words 1–6 in sentences using the "ing" form.

example: **We were hurrying to be on time.**

• Use words 7–12 in sentences using the "ed" form.

example: **Father replied to the newspaper ad.**

Wednesday

• Use words 1–6 in sentences using the "ed" form.

  example: **We hurried, but we were too late.**

• Use words 7–12 in sentences using the "ing" form.

  example: **Father is replying by letter.**

Thursday

For six of your spelling words, write sentences containing two forms (base word, "ing," or "ed") of the spelling word.

example: **I hurried to school, but I don't like hurrying.**

Verb Review

Name _____ Week_____

Rule: Remember to make spelling changes to verbs when adding "ed" and "ing."

Verb (base word)	*Verb + ed*	*Verb + ing*
1. _____	_____	_____
2. _____	_____	_____
3. _____	_____	_____
4. _____	_____	_____
5. _____	_____	_____
6. _____	_____	_____
7. _____	_____	_____
8. _____	_____	_____

Monday

- Use words 1–4 in questions using the "ed" form of the verb.
- Use words 5–8 in questions using the "ing" form of the verb.
- Write all base words two times.

Tuesday

- Use words 1–4 in statements using the "ing" form of the verb.
- Use words 5–8 in statements using the "ed" form of the verb.
- Write all base words in letter boxes.
  example: 🄣 🄗 🄘 🄝 🄚

Wednesday

- Look up words 1–4 in the dictionary and write all forms of the verb found at the end of the entry.
- Write the "ed" and "ing" forms of words 5–8 and circle all spelling changes.
  example: **hop**   **hops**   **ho(pp)ed**   **ho(pp)ing**

Thursday

- Look up words 5–8 and write all forms of the verb found.
- Write "ed" and "ing" forms of words 1–4 and circle any spelling changes.

"F" Sound Made by "PH" and "GH"

Name _____ Week_____

(**Teacher Note:** *See page 127 for appropriate words.*)

1. _____   7. _____
2. _____   8. _____
3. _____   9. _____
4. _____   10. _____
5. _____   11. _____
6. _____   12. _____

Monday

Write each spelling word two times normally. Write each one again, capitalizing the "ph" or "gh" in each word.

example: **trophy trophy troPHy**

laugh laugh lauGH

Tuesday

• Write sentences using spelling words 1 and 2 together, 3 and 4 together, and 5 and 6 together in the same sentences.

example: **Jason did not <u>laugh</u> at the giant <u>trophy</u>.**

• Write spelling words 7–12. Look up these words in the dictionary and write their phonetic spellings.

example: **rough   (ruf)**

Wednesday

• Write spelling words 1–6. Look up these words in the dictionary and write down their phonetic spellings.

• Write sentences by using spelling words 7 and 8 together, 9 and 10, and 11 and 12 together in the same sentences.

Thursday

Copy the headings below and place each spelling word under the correct heading, according to where the "f" sound is found in each of the words.

Beginning of Word	**Middle of Word**	**End of Word**
<u>ph</u>oto	tro<u>ph</u>y	lau<u>gh</u>

Soft "G" Sound Words

Name _____ Week_____

> **Rule:** When the letter "g" is followed by the letters "e," "i," or "y," it usually makes the soft "g" sound like the letter "j."

(**Teacher Note:** *See page 127 for appropriate words.*)

1. _____   7. _____
2. _____   8. _____
3. _____   9. _____
4. _____   10. _____
5. _____   11. _____
6. _____   12. _____

Monday ─────────────────────────

Write your spelling words one time normally and then one time circling the letter "g" and the letter "e," "i," or "y" that follows.

example: **gentle**   **(ge)ntle**

Tuesday ─────────────────────────

Write each spelling word and then look up its phonetic spelling in the dictionary and write it.

example: **gentle**   **(jent´l)**

Wednesday ─────────────────────────

Write each spelling word in a sentence using several words that actually begin with a "j."

example: **Jerry was gentle as he handled Julie's jewelry.**

Thursday ─────────────────────────

Write your spelling words in alphabetical order. You may need to look at the third or fourth letters in each word because there may be several words that begin with "ge," "gi," or "gy."

Soft "C" Sound Words

Name _____   Week_____

> **Rule:** When the letter "c" is followed by the letters "e," "i," or "y," it usually makes the soft "c" sound like the letter "s."

(**Teacher Note:** *See page 127 for appropriate words.*)

1. _____   7. _____
2. _____   8. _____
3. _____   9. _____
4. _____   10. _____
5. _____   11. _____
6. _____   12. _____

Monday

Write each spelling word one time normally and then one time capitalizing the letters "ce," "ci," or "cy."

example: **cycle   CYcle**

                 city   CIty

Tuesday

Think of a word that is actually spelled with the letter "s" that goes with each spelling word or can describe it somehow.

example: **cycle   spin**

                 city   subway

Wednesday

Take the words from Tuesday's lesson and make a sentence from each pair. Underline each spelling word.

example: **The washer is on the spin <u>cycle</u>.**

           We rode the subway into the <u>city</u>.

Thursday

Write your spelling words in alphabetical order. You may need to use the third and fourth letters in some of your words to do so.

"QU" and "SQU" Words

Name _____ Week_____

| **Rule:** The letter "q" is always followed by the letter "u." |

(**Teacher Note:** *See page 128 for appropriate words.*)

1. _____
2. _____
3. _____
4. _____
5. _____
6. _____

7. _____
8. _____
9. _____
10. _____
11. _____
12. _____

Monday

Write each spelling word two times normally and then one time by writing the "qu" or "squ" letters in red and the rest in pencil.

Tuesday

Write your spelling words in alphabetical order. Be careful because you may have to use the third or fourth letters to do so.

Wednesday

Write a sentence for each spelling word. Include a contraction in each sentence somewhere. Underline each spelling word.

example: **Shouldn't we bow before the <u>queen</u>?**

I can't <u>quit</u> until the job is finished.

Thursday

Write each spelling word. Look each word up in your dictionary and write down what part of speech it is (how it can be used).

example: **queen (*noun*)**

quit (*verb*)

Changing "F" to "VES" When Plural

Name _____ Week_____

> **Rule:** Words ending in "f" or "fe" are changed to "ves" when made plural.

(**Teacher Note:** *See page 128 for appropriate words.*)

1. _____   6. _____
2. _____   7. _____
3. _____   8. _____
4. _____   9. _____
5. _____   10. _____

Monday

Write each spelling word in its singular form and its plural form.

Underline the "f" and circle the "ves."

example: **half   hal ves**

Tuesday

- Draw pictures illustrating spelling words 1–5, both as singular and plural.

example: **half   halves**

- Write sentences for words 6–10 using both singular and plural forms of each word in each sentence.

example: **The wolf ran in a pack with other wolves.**

Wednesday

- Write sentences for words 1–5 using both singular and plural forms of each word in each sentence.

- Draw pictures illustrating both singular and plural forms of spelling words 6–10.

Thursday

Write each spelling word's plural form horizontally and connect its singular form vertically by sharing the same beginning letter.

example: **halves**

    a

    l

    f

Irregular Plural Nouns

Name _____   Week_____

> **Rule:** Some nouns create new words when showing more than one.
> Some nouns use the same word for singular and plural forms.

(**Teacher Note:** *See page 128 for appropriate words.*)

1. _____   7. _____
2. _____   8. _____
3. _____   9. _____
4. _____   10. _____
5. _____   11. _____
6. _____   12. _____

Monday

Write each noun and its plural form side by side. Underline the letters in the singular form that you also find in the plural form.

example: <u>m</u>ous<u>e</u>   mice

Tuesday

• Write sentences for words 1–6 using the singular forms of each word.

example: **The mouse ran into the hole in the floor.**

• Write sentences for words 7–12 using the plural forms of each word.

example: **My books fit neatly on the shelves.**

Wednesday

Write the singular form of each spelling word horizontally and the plural form of each word vertically, sharing the same beginning letter.

example: **mouse**
       i
       c
       e

Thursday

Write sentences using the singular form and plural form of each word in the same sentence.

example: **The mouse lived with other mice in the garden.**

Double Consonants

Name _____ *Week* _____

Rule: Words with double consonants are divided into syllables between the consonants.

(**Teacher Note:** *See page 129 for appropriate words.*)

1. _____
2. _____
3. _____
4. _____
5. _____
6. _____

7. _____
8. _____
9. _____
10. _____
11. _____
12. _____

Monday

Write each spelling word in pencil, again in pen, and one more time in pencil.

Tuesday

- Write spelling words 1–6 and ⟨circle⟩ the double consonants. Look up these words in a dictionary and copy the word as it is divided into syllables (found at the end of each entry).

  example: **ba ⟨ll⟩ oon** (bal loon)

- Write spelling words 7–12 and give your own definition of the word. Do not use the dictionary for this part!

  example: **balloon**—a round stretchy object you can blow up with air

Wednesday

- Write spelling words 1–6 and your own definitions of these words.
- Write words 7–12 and ⟨circle⟩ the double consonants. Use the dictionary to copy the way each word is divided into syllables.

Thursday

Write the spelling list in alphabetical order. Write each word again using capital letters for the double consonants.

example: **balloons   baLLoons**

Words with Digraphs

Name _____ Week_____

Rule: Digraphs are the letter combinations "ch," "sh," "th," and "wh." The two letters work together to make only one sound.

(**Teacher Note:** *See page 129 for appropriate words.*)

1. _____	7. _____
2. _____	8. _____
3. _____	9. _____
4. _____	10. _____
5. _____	11. _____
6. _____	12. _____

Monday

Write each spelling word. Write it again and circle the digraph.

example: **shadow**   (sh) **adow**

earth   **ear** (th)

Tuesday

Write each spelling word and then label two boxes **Beginning Digraph** and **Ending Digraph**. Place each spelling word in the correct box on your paper.
example:

Beginning Digraph	Ending Digraph
shadow chew	earth

Wednesday

Write each spelling word in a sentence that uses an abbreviation.
example: **I saw my shadow on Main St.**
Mrs. Brewer is teaching about earth.
Chew your Mr. Goodbar before it melts.

Thursday

Write each spelling word three times and star your neatest writing for each of the words.

Words That Add "ES"

Name _____ Week _____

Rule: Words that end in "ch," "s," "sh," "ss," "zz," and "x" add "es" to the end.

(**Teacher Note:** *See page 130 for appropriate words.*)

1. _____   7. _____
2. _____   8. _____
3. _____   9. _____
4. _____   10. _____
5. _____   11. _____
6. _____   12. _____

Monday

Write the base word of each spelling word. Write each word again, capitalizing the "ch," "s," "sh," "ss," "zz," or "x" at the end of each base word. Now write each spelling word with "es" on the end.

example: **watch   watCH   watches**

Tuesday

• Write sentences for words 1–6 using the base words.

example: **Fred can watch for the school bus out his window.**

• Write sentences for words 7–12 after adding "es" to the end.

example: **Mrs. Jackson wishes she had taken an earlier train.**

Wednesday

• Write sentences for words 1–6 after adding "es" to the end.
example: **Mr. Jackson watches football every Sunday.**
• Write sentences for words 7–12 using the base words.
example: **I wish I had an older sister.**

Thursday

Use a Venn diagram to organize your spelling words. Label the diagram **Used as a Noun** on the left, **Used as a Verb** on the right, and **Used as a Noun or a Verb** in the middle.

Common Syllables

Name _____ Week _____

> **Rule:** Common syllables are letter groups found at the beginning of many words. Some beginning common syllables are "be" . . . and "a" . . .

(**Teacher Note:** *See page 130 for appropriate words.*)

1. _____   7. _____
2. _____   8. _____
3. _____   9. _____
4. _____   10. _____
5. _____   11. _____
6. _____   12. _____

Monday

Write each spelling word two times in pencil and one time in pen. Circle the beginning common syllables.

Tuesday

- Write words 1–6 normally and then in "smiley faces."

example:

- Write words 7–12 in sentences and include names of characters from fairy tales you have read. Underline the spelling word.

example: **Cinderella had to work <u>alone</u> every day.**

Wednesday

- Write words 1–6 in sentences using the names of teachers you know. Circle the spelling word.

example: **Mrs. Green teaches (beside) Mrs. Smith.**

- Write words 7–12 normally and then in "smiley faces."

Thursday

Look up each spelling word in a dictionary. Write each spelling word and then copy the word as it is divided into syllables (look at the pronunciation at the end of the entry).

example: **away** (a way)   **before** (be fore)

Words with Suffixes

Name _____   Week_____

> **Rule:** A suffix is a common syllable added to the end of an existing word or base word. A suffix changes the meaning of the base word.

(**Teacher Note:** *See page 131 for appropriate words.*)

1. _____   7. _____
2. _____   8. _____
3. _____   9. _____
4. _____   10. _____
5. _____   11. _____
6. _____   12. _____

Monday

Write each spelling word. Write them again underlining the base words and circling the suffixes.

example: **tasteless**   taste (less)
          hopeful   hope (ful)
          appointment   appoint (ment)

Tuesday

Write each spelling word in a complete sentence telling the word's meaning.

example: **Tasteless means having no taste.**
          To be hopeful is to have hope.
          An appointment is a meeting at a certain time.

Wednesday

Write each base word. Write each spelling word next to its base word. Then write other forms of the word with suffixes that you can think of.

example: **taste**   **tasteless**   **tasty**
          hope   **hopeful**   **hopeless**
          appoint   **appointment**   **appointing**

Thursday

Write a sentence using each spelling word.

example: **This meatloaf is <u>tasteless</u>.**
          Sharon is <u>hopeful</u> she will be picked for the play.
          Don't be late for your <u>appointment</u>.

Words with Prefixes

Name _____ Week_____

> **Rule:** Prefixes are letters or letter groups that are added to the beginning of a word (base word) to make a new word. Some prefixes are "un," "re," "mis," and "dis."

(**Teacher Note:** *See page 131 for appropriate words.*)

1. _____   7. _____
2. _____   8. _____
3. _____   9. _____
4. _____   10. _____
5. _____   11. _____
6. _____   12. _____

Monday

Write each spelling word. Then write the base word without the prefix. Next, write the spelling word and circle the prefix with a crayon.

example: **unhappy   happy (un) happy**

Tuesday

Write words 1–6 in sentences first with the prefixes and then with only the base words.

example: **My mother was unhappy. Clowns make me happy.**

For words 7–12 write prefix + base word = spelling word.

example: **un + happy = unhappy**

Wednesday

For words 1–6 write prefix + base word = spelling word.

Write words 7–12 in sentences first with the prefixes and then with only the base words.

Thursday

In a dictionary, look up the base words for the spelling list. Write the base word and then any other word forms you find at the end of each dictionary entry.

example: **happy, *unhappy, happier, happiest***

Comparative Endings

Name _____ Week_____

> **Rule:** To make an adjective compare two things, add "er" to the end. If the adjective ends with "y," change the "y" to an "i" and then add "er."

(**Teacher Note:** *See page 132 for appropriate words.*)

1. _____ 7. _____

2. _____ 8. _____

3. _____ 9. _____

4. _____ 10. _____

5. _____ 11. _____

6. _____ 12. _____

Monday

Write each adjective one time. Write the "er" form of each word two times and (circle) each new "i" with a red pen.

Tuesday

- Write sentences for words 1–6. Use both forms of the word in the sentence. <u>Underline</u> each word.

  example: **Your dog is <u>lazy</u>, but my dog is <u>*lazier*</u>.**

- Look up base words 7–12 in the dictionary. Write the word, the page number, and all other forms of the word found in the entry.

Wednesday

- Write sentences for words 7–12 using both forms of the word (same as Tuesday's directions for 1–6).

- Look up words 1–6 in the dictionary. Write the base word, page number, and all forms of the word found.

Thursday

- Draw and color pictures to illustrate at least four of the word pairs from your list.

  example: **Draw a picture of something *long* and then something *longer*.**

Adverbs

Name _____ Week _____

> **Rule:** Adverbs tell more about a verb. They can tell when, where, or how. (Examples: She raced *yesterday*. The hat blew *away*. The man spoke *softly*.)

(**Teacher Note:** *See page 132 for appropriate words.*)

1. _____   7. _____
2. _____   8. _____
3. _____   9. _____
4. _____   10. _____
5. _____   11. _____
6. _____   12. _____

Monday

Write each adverb two times and then write a verb you think would be used with each adverb.

example: **up   up   *floated***

Tuesday

- Write sentences for adverbs 1–6. <u>Underline</u> the verb in each sentence and circle your adverb in each sentence.

example: **The balloon <u>floated</u> (up) in the sky.**

- Write adverbs 7–12 and then tell if they describe when, where, or how.

example: **there** (where)   **early** (when)   **slowly** (how)

Wednesday

- Write adverbs 1–6 and then tell whether they describe when, where, or how.

example: **inside** (where)   **yesterday** (when)   **softly** (how)

Thursday

- Write all adverbs in alphabetical order.
- Then choose four of the adverbs to write in sentences.
- Draw a picture to illustrate each of the sentences.

Pronouns

Name _____ Week _____

Rule: Pronouns are words that take the place of nouns. They can be singular, plural, and/or possessive.

(**Teacher Note:** *See page 132 for appropriate words.*)

1. _____   7. _____
2. _____   8. _____
3. _____   9. _____
4. _____   10. _____
5. _____   11. _____
6. _____   12. _____

Monday

Write each spelling word under the correct heading. Some words may be written under more than one heading.

example:

Singular	**Plural**	**Possessive**
I	we	our

Tuesday

Write a sentence for all the pronouns that can be used in the subject of a sentence. Don't forget the possessive pronouns!

example: **I can go to the movies on Saturday.**

We have a baseball game tomorrow.

Our class will have pictures taken soon.

Wednesday

Write a sentence for all the pronouns that can be used in the predicate of a sentence. Remember those possessive pronouns.

example: **That book belongs to me.**

The teacher will return their book reports.

Thursday

Use a Venn diagram to organize your pronouns. Label the left side **Use in Subject**, right side, **Use in Predicate**, and the center **Use in Subject and Predicate.**

Homophones

Name _____ Week_____

> **Rule:** Homophones are words that sound the same but have different meanings and spellings.

(**Teacher Note:** *See page 133 for appropriate words.*)

1. _____   7. _____

2. _____   8. _____

3. _____   9. _____

4. _____   10. _____

5. _____   11. _____

6. _____   12. _____

Monday

Write each spelling word two times in pencil and then two times in red pen. Be careful . . . make no mistakes!

Tuesday

- Look up words 1–6 in the dictionary. Write the sentence used in the entry. <u>Underline</u> the spelling word.

- Write spelling words 7–12 and save room in front of the words to write the entry word that comes before the spelling word on the dictionary page. Then write the entry word that comes after the spelling word.

     example: **lake**   **lamb**   **lame**

Wednesday

- Do just the opposite of what you did yesterday. Write spelling words 1–6 with the entry words before and after each one.

- Write the sentences from the dictionary for words 7–12. Don't forget to <u>underline</u> your spelling words!

Thursday

Write your own sentences for all of the spelling words. Be careful to use them correctly!

Contractions

Name _____ Week _____

> **Rule:** Contractions are made by combining two words and shortening them by using an apostrophe to make one word.

(**Teacher Note:** *See page 134 for appropriate words.*)

1. _____   7. _____
2. _____   8. _____
3. _____   9. _____
4. _____   10. _____
5. _____   11. _____
6. _____   12. _____

Monday

Write each contraction three times. (Circle) your neatest try for each word.

Tuesday

Make a chart and label four columns—**Contraction, Word One, Word Two,** and **Letters Removed.**

Fill in the chart for each of your spelling words.

example:

Contraction	Word One	Word Two	Letters Removed
can't	can	not	n, o

Wednesday

- Use spelling words 1–6 in sentences.
- Write words 7–12 and then look them up in your dictionary and write the page number on which you found each contraction.

example:

can't—page 48 _____
                                            title of your dictionary

Thursday

- Write words 1–6 and their dictionary page numbers.
- Use spelling words 7–12 in sentences.

Compound Words

Name _____ Week _____

Rule: A compound word is a new word made from combining (but not changing) two existing words.

(**Teacher Note:** *See page 134 for appropriate words.*)

1. _____ 7. _____

2. _____ 8. _____

3. _____ 9. _____

4. _____ 10. _____

5. _____ 11. _____

6. _____ 12. _____

Monday

Write each compound word one time normally. Then write each compound word using a pencil for the first word and a pen for the second word.

Tuesday

- Write words 1–6 and beside each spelling word try to write a new compound word made up from one of the two words used in your spelling word.

  example: **mailman**   **mailbox**

- Use words 7–12 in sentences. Draw a box around each spelling word.

Wednesday

- Use words 1–6 in commands. Draw a circle around each spelling word.

- Write words 7–12. Beside each spelling word try to write a new compound word made from one of the words in your spelling word.

Thursday

Make a three-column chart for your compound spelling words. Label **Word One, Word Two**, and **Compound Word.** Fill in the chart with each of your spelling words.

example:

Word One	Word Two	Compound Word
mail	man	mailman

Focus on Syllables (1)

Name _____ *Week* _____

> **Rule:** All words can be divided into parts or syllables. Each syllable has one vowel sound. The vowel sounds may be long, short, "r" controlled, dipthongs, or schwas.

(**Teacher Note:** *See page 135 for appropriate words.*)

1. _____
2. _____
3. _____
4. _____
5. _____
6. _____

7. _____
8. _____
9. _____
10. _____
11. _____
12. _____

Monday

Write each spelling word two times and place a star next to your neatest writing of each word.

Tuesday

• Write words 1–6 and then use your dictionary to divide each word into syllables.

example: **umpire   um pire**

• Write sentences for words 7–12. Include a proper noun in each of your sentences. <u>Underline</u> your spelling word.

example: **I have <u>never</u> vacationed in Arizona.**

Wednesday

• Write a sentence for each of words 1–6. Include a compound word in each of your sentences. Underline your spelling word.

example: **The <u>umpire</u> was late getting to the ballgame.**

• Write words 7–12 and use your dictionary to divide each word into syllables.

Thursday

Write each of your spelling words as syllable puzzle pieces that lock together. Rewrite each word correctly and circle the vowel sound heard in each syllable.

example: | un ⟩ der ⟩ stand | ⓤn dⓔr stⓐnd

Focus on Syllables (2)

Name _____ Week_____

> **Rule:** All words can be divided into parts or syllables. Each syllable has one vowel sound. The vowel sound may be long, short, "r" controlled, dipthongs, or schwas.

(**Teacher Note:** *See page 135 for appropriate words.*)

1. _____   7. _____

2. _____   8. _____

3. _____   9. _____

4. _____   10. _____

5. _____   11. _____

6. _____   12. _____

Monday

Write each spelling word one time in print and one time in cursive.

Tuesday

- Write words 1–6 in sentences in narrative form. Use different names of family members for the speakers in each sentence.

  example: **Robert said, "Get the umbrella because it is raining."**

- Write words 7–12 and then use your dictionary to divide each word into syllables. Circle the stressed syllable in each word.

  example: **victory**   (vic) tor y

Wednesday

- Write words 1–6. Use your dictionary again to divide each word into syllables. Circle the stressed syllable.

  example: **umbrella**   um (brel) la

- Write a short paragraph about a shopping spree. Include spelling words 7–12 in your paragraph. Underline each spelling word.

Thursday

Write each of your spelling words and then another word that shares one of the same syllables as that spelling word. Draw a [box] around the matching syllables found in both words.

  examples: [um] brella   [um] pire

  yes [ter] day   sis [ter]

Section Four

Management
(Forms, Diagrams,
Word Lists, Glossary)

Weekly Spelling Record

Date Name	Activities	Test	Activities	Test	Activities	Test	Activities	Test	Activities	Test	Activities	Test	Activities	Test	Activities	Test	Activities	Test	Activities	Test

Word Search Form A

Name _____ Week_____

Word Box

Hide the word list above in the letter boxes below, going in any direction.
Fill in any leftover boxes with other letters of the alphabet.
Have a friend or family member circle each word as he or she finds it.

Write here each word found in your word search above.

Word Search Form B

Name _____ *Week*_____

Word Bank

These are the spelling words hidden in the word search below.

Write the words from the word bank in the puzzle below. Fill in the empty boxes with alphabet letters.

Now go back and circle each spelling word with a crayon or red pen. You can help your mother, father, brother, or sister try to find them!

Venn Diagram

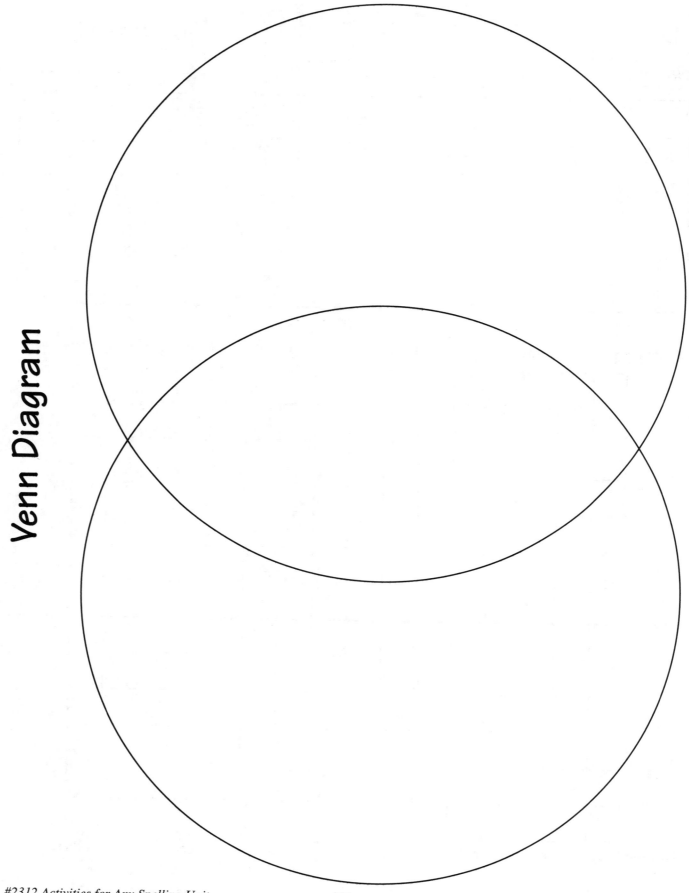

Specific Skills Word Lists

Short Vowel Word Families 1 (page 83)

back	bag	can	bat
jack	gag	Dan	cat
lack	lag	fan	fat
pack	nag	Jan	hat
quack	rag	man	mat
rack	sag	pan	pat
sack	tag	ran	rat
tack	wag	tan	sat
black	brag	van	vat
crack	drag	bran	flat
stack	flag	clan	scat
track		plan	chat
snack		than	that

bad	am	cap	bass
dad	dam	gap	lass
fad	ham	lap	mass
had	jam	map	pass
lad	Pam	nap	brass
mad	ram	rap	class
pad	Sam	sap	glass
sad	tam	tap	grass
Tad	yan	zap	
clad	gram	clap	
glad		flap	
		snap	
		trap	

bed	bell	Ben	bet
fed	dell	den	get
red	fell	hen	jet
Ted	sell	men	let
wed	tell	pen	met
fled	well	ten	net
Fred	yell	wren	pet
shed	smell	then	set
	spell	when	vet
	swell		wet
	shell		yet

Specific Skills Word Lists *(cont.)*

Short Vowel Word Families 2 (page 83)

best	bill	will	pin
jest	dill	drill	tin
nest	fill	skill	win
quest	hill	spill	chin
rest	Jill	still	thin
test	kill	thrill	shin
vest	mill	bin	bit
west	pill	din	fit
zest	quill	fin	hit
crest	sill	kin	kit

lit	sip	mop	dot
pit	tip	pop	got
quit	zip	top	hot
sit	drip	crop	jot
knit	flip	drop	lot
slit	snip	flop	not
dip	trip	plop	pot
hip	ship	stop	tot
lip	whip	shop	spot
rip	hop	cot	slot

trot	bun	jug	club
dock	fun	mug	grub
lock	gun	rug	buck
rock	nun	tug	duck
sock	run	plug	luck
block	sun	cub	muck
clock	spun	hub	suck
flock	stun	rub	tuck
knock	bug	sub	pluck
stock	dug	tub	stuck
shock	hug	stub	truck

Specific Skills Word Lists *(cont.)*

Long Vowel Word Families 1 (page 83)

bay	tray	take	rate
day	bake	wake	skate
hay	cake	flake	plate
may	fake	shake	ace
pay	Jake	ate	face
say	lake	date	lace
way	make	gate	pace
play	quake	Kate	race
stay	rake	late	grace
gray	sake	mate	place

space	rail	same	tree
trace	sail	tame	three
bail	tail	blame	flee
Gail	snail	frame	be
hail	trail	shame	he
jail	came	bee	me
mail	fame	fee	we
nail	game	knee	deed
pail	lame	see	feed
quail	name	wee	need

reed	peep	seat	scream
seed	weep	treat	stream
weed	steep	wheat	feel
bleed	sweep	beam	heel
greed	sheep	seam	kneel
speed	beat	team	peel
beep	eat	cream	reel
deep	heat	dream	steel
jeep	meat	gleam	wheel
keep	neat	steam	

Specific Skills Word Lists (cont.)

Long Vowel Word Families 2 (page 83)

beet	sheet	spice	pride
feet	dice	twice	slide
meet	ice	hide	stride
fleet	mice	ride	fight
greet	nice	side	light
sleet	rice	tide	might
sweet	price	wide	night
street	slice	bride	right

sight	pine	fold	boat
tight	vine	gold	coat
bright	wine	hold	goat
dine	spine	mold	moat
fine	shine	old	oat
line	whine	sold	float
mine	bold	told	gloat
nine	cold	scold	throat

joke	stroke	grow	tune
poke	bow	show	cute
woke	low	throw	mute
yoke	mow	fuse	flute
broke	row	muse	suit
choke	tow	use	fruit
smoke	blow	dune	
spoke	flow	June	

Specific Skills Word Lists *(cont.)*

Two Vowels Go Walking! Words (page 84)

ea	ei	ai	oa	ie
team	ceiling	rain	toast	pie
clean	seize	sail	coat	tried
leaf	protein	gait	boat	cried
seam	neither	nail	coal	pliers
lean	either	train	float	science
dream	deceive	paint	goat	die
mean	leisure	wait	roam	quiet
steam	receive	rail	roast	spied
neat	conceited	stain	soak	implied
beam	deceit	drain	boast	dried

Vowel-Consonant-Silent "E" Words (page 85)

These make the long vowel sound and drop the "e" before adding an ending.

Long a	Long i	Long o	Long u
cake	file	robe	cute
late	time	home	rude
fake	dime	stove	use
tame	kite	close	fumes
blame	smile	hope	huge
state	nice	nose	plume
rake	dive	rope	June
bake	bike	drove	crude
space	drive	woke	mute
save	slide	stone	mule
name	price	wrote	tube
place	size	hose	yule

Specific Skills word Lists (cont.)

"R"-Controlled Words (page 86)

-ar	-ard	-are	-ark	-arm
car	card	bare	bark	arm
far	yard	care	dark	farm
jar	lard	dare	lark	harm
tar		hare	mark	charm
star		rare	park	
scar		blare	spark	
		stare	shark	

-arn	-arp	-art	-ear	-eer
barn	carp	art	dear	deer
yarn	harp	cart	fear	jeer
darn	tarp	dart	gear	cheer
	sharp	part	hear	sheer
		smart	near	steer
		start	spear	
			bear	
			tear	
			wear	

-ir	-ire	-irt	-or	-ord
fir	fire	dirt	for	cord
stir	tire	shirt	nor	Ford
sir	wire	squirt	story	sword
whirl	spire	flirt	glory	word
swirl		skirt		
girl				

-ore	-ork	-orn	-ort	-urt	-ur
core	cork	corn	fort	hurt	fur
sore	fork	born	port	curt	purr
more	pork	morn	sort	blurt	blur
tore	stork	torn	sport		urn
score	work	worn	short		burn
snore		scorn	snort		turn
chore		thorn			
store					

Specific Skills Word Lists *(cont.)*

"Y" Within Words (page 87)

That Make the Long "i" Sound				That Make Other Sounds		
hydrant	python	type		lyric	syringe	myriad
cycle	hyena	hygiene		cyst	mystery	mystify
typhoon	cyclone	dynasty				
bylaw	pylon	gyrate				
hype	hyphen	tyrant				

"EI" Words (page 88)

deceive	conceited	receipt	deceitful
ceiling	freight	weight	deign
reign	beige	their	feign
either	height	foreign	seize
protein	heir	veil	eight
neighbor	vein	weigh	sleigh
neither	weird	seine	receive

"IE" Words (page 89)

brief	chief	thief	grief
science	audience	believe	relief
convenient	experience	friend	shriek
die	fierce	field	quiet
piece	conscience	hierarchy	variety
efficient	fiesta	niece	belief
pier	piece	ancient	proficient
sufficient	briefly	disbelief	grieve

Specific Skills Word Lists *(cont.)*

Verbs That Drop the Silent "E" (page 90)
When Adding "ING" or "ED"

care	race	store	bake	hope
file	rake	tame	grade	space
scrape	scare	smile	shape	move
shove	love	paste	waste	erase
close	state	dare	hate	rope
live	exchange	arrive	compare	replace
move	change	serve	name	reserve

Verbs That Double the Last Consonant (page 91)
When Adding "ING" or "ED"

hop	trot	stop	grab	sip
hum	jog	rip	rub	slam
pet	step	tap	chat	flog
grin	stab	trap	shop	snap

Words Ending in "Y" (page 92)

Verbs			**Adjectives**		
hurry	reply	stay	pretty	heavy	silly
fry	worry	pray	lonely	lazy	funny
cry	scurry	destroy	fancy	angry	lovely
pry	bury	employ			
study	play		thirsty	easy	
carry	enjoy				

Specific Skills Word Lists *(cont.)*

"F" Sound Made By "PH" and "GH" (page 94)

"PH" Words

photo	trophy	orphan
alphabet	dolphin	elephant
nephew	phrase	
phony	telephone	

"GH" Words

enough	graph	laugh
rough	cough	tough

Soft "G" Sound Words (page 95)

"GE"		"GI"		"GY"
gentle	strange	ginger	margin	gym
gem	average	gigantic	fragile	gypsy
genuine	surgery	giraffe	regiment	gymnast
fudge	gorgeous	giant	garage	gymnasium
gently	general	register	gingerly	gypsum
angel	gelatin	magic	hinge	gyro
				gyrate

Soft "C" Sound Words (page 96)

"CE"		"CI"		"CY"
cellar	celebrate	city	cider	cycle
certain	cereal	circle	circuit	cyclist
ceiling	central	circular	citrus	cyclone
ceremony	certificate	circus	cirrus	encyclopedia
cent	century	citizen	cinema	cymbal
center	centipede	circulate	cigar	cynical
				cypress
				cyst

Specific Skills Word Lists (cont.)

"QU" and "SQU" Words (page 97)

"QU"		**"SQU"**	
quack	quad	squeak	squid
quarter	quadrangle	squash	squaw
queen	quake	squirrel	squiggle
question	quail	squeamish	squint
quickly	Quaker	squawk	squelch
quiet	qualify	squeal	squirt
quietly	quartz	square	squander
quite	quiver	squad	squirm
quilt	quart	squabble	squire
quill		squeeze	

"F" to "VES" Words (page 98)

half	knife	loaf	life	elf
wife	wolf	calf	shelf	leaf

Nouns with Irregular Plurals (page 99)

man	men	elf	elves
woman	women	calf	calves
foot	feet	wolf	wolves
tooth	teeth	leaf	leaves
mouse	mice	loaf	loaves
ox	oxen	wife	wives
goose	geese	knife	knives
		shelf	shelves
		scarf	scarves

Words with the Same Plurals

fish	deer	sheep

Specific Skills Word Lists *(cont.)*

Words with Double Consonants (page 100)

yellow	puppy	common	rubber
butter	letter	balloon	hammer
summer	buzzer	better	willow
rudder	setter	sitter	spelling
fritter	pillow	bunny	winner
sunny	bonnet	fellow	paddle
manners	barrette	glitter	cotton
lettuce	banner	hello	critter
puppet	puddle	runner	busses
patter	ballot	mallet	mellow

Beginning and Ending Digraph Words (page 101)

ch-	-ch	sh-	-sh
chair	bench	shoe	dish
chain	touch	shell	fish
chew	watch	shirt	rash
cherry	catch	shop	splash
chore	punch	shore	trash
chirp	scratch	she	crush
churn	lunch	shadow	plush
chisel	such	ship	radish
chocolate	pouch	shower	punish
chin	each	shovel	flush
chunk	roach	shoulder	push
choice	flinch	shout	ash

th-		-th		wh-	
that	these	fifth	sloth	wheel	whistle
their	thimble	math	earth	when	whale
this	think	bath	booth	where	wharf
them	thought	cloth	hearth	whirl	what
thumb	through	sixth	smooth	which	whisker
thorn	threw	both	tooth	whip	wheeze

Specific Skills Word Lists (cont.)

Words That Add "ES" to the End (page 102)

> Words that end in "ch," "s," "ss," "sh," "zz," and "x" add "es" to the end.

-ch	-s	-sh	-zz
match	bus	dish	buzz
watch	gas	wash	fizz
catch		splash	
torch	**-ss**	radish	**-x**
touch	miss	push	ax
scratch	pass	fish	fax
lunch	kiss	crush	box
bench	dress	wish	
punch	caress	push	

Common Beginning Syllables (page 103)

a		be	
about	above	bewilder	became
alone	across	begin	began
aboard	ajar	between	beneath
able	awake	before	beware
afloat	aware	beside	behalf
away	alive	below	behind
again	agree	because	beyond
anew		become	behold
apart			

Specific Skills Word Lists *(cont.)*

Words with Suffixes (page 104)

-ful	**-less**	**-ment**	**-ness**
helpful	careless	argument	happiness
beautiful	penniless	government	forgetfulness
careful	senseless	measurement	roughness
plentiful	hopeless	arrangement	kindness
tasteful	tasteless	appointment	kindliness
hopeful	motionless	judgement	sweetness
bountiful	helpless	assignment	seriousness
fanciful	useless	advertisement	darkness

-ly	**-er**	**-able**	**-y**
loudly	helper	likeable	shiny
softly	runner	changeable	windy
quickly	teacher	remarkable	lengthy
slowly	painter	agreeable	mighty
nicely	swimmer	lovable	pointy
surprisingly	photographer	predictable	sunny
happily	driver	unforgettable	lucky
neatly	reporter	uncontrollable	frosty

Words with Prefixes (page 105)

re-	**mis-**	**un-**	**de-**
rewrite	mistake	unhappy	defrost
recall	misunderstand	unreal	decode
rearrange	misfortune	unwind	depress
remove	misguide	untie	degrade
replay	misfire	unprepared	depart
remodel	mislead	unfortunate	delight
rebuild	misadvise	unwilling	denote
repay	mismatch	unhelpful	derail
reset	mistook	unhealthy	despite
recycle	mislead	unusual	detour

Specific Skills Word Lists *(cont.)*

Adjectives That End With "Y" (page 106)

silly	crazy	friendly
sunny	fuzzy	easy
shiny	rainy	angry
fancy	pretty	early
busy	lonely	lazy
funny	juicy	hungry

Adverbs (page 107)

When	Where	How
now	here	quickly
soon	there	slowly
later	around	nicely
finally	near	smoothly
often	under	remarkably
always	beside	quietly
never	over	softly
early	up	sweetly
briefly	down	warmly
tomorrow	everywhere	busily
already	nearby	rapidly

Pronouns (page 108)

Used in Subject	Used in Predicate	Possessive
I	me	my, mine
you	you	your, yours
he	him	his
she	her	her
it	it	its
we	us	our, ours
they	them	their, theirs

Specific Skills Word Lists (cont.)

Homophones (page 109)

Homophones are words that are pronounced the same, have different meanings, and are spelled differently.

bear	bare		hair	hare
flour	flower		sea	see
I	eye		right	write
wear	where		cent	sent
their	there	they're	ewe	you
blue	blew		plain	plane
or	ore		tail	tale
gate	gait		ale	ail
gym	Jim		be	bee
bow	beau		deer	dear
sell	cell		so	sew
do	dew		for	four
sail	sale		heel	heal
hi	high		lay	lei
jamb	jam		meet	meat
lent	Lent		pale	pail
need	knead		no	know
knew	new		pain	pane
fourth	forth		rain	reign
prey	pray		too	two	to
road	rode		red	read
pore	pour		hole	whole
son	sun		urn	earn
wait	weight		one	won
vane	vein		dye	die
toe	tow		sweet	suite

Specific Skills Word Lists (cont.)

Contractions (page 110)

I'm	I'll	I've	you'll	you've
he's	he'll	she's	she'll	they'll
they've	we'll	we've	it's	I'd
you'd	he'd	she'd	they'd	we'd
you're	they're	we're	it'll	
aren't	can't	couldn't	doesn't	hasn't
haven't	isn't	wasn't	weren't	won't
shouldn't	don't	hadn't	wouldn't	didn't

Compound Words (page 111)

baseball	anytime	raindrop	sundress
ballpark	sailboat	anywhere	airplane
snowball	boathouse	playtime	motorboat
pinball	rowboat	sometime	hardhat
mailman	lifeboat	timekeeper	washcloth
mailbox	manhole	boxcar	soapsuds
daylight	snowman	sundial	treehouse
today	storybook	bedroom	tophat
someday	bookstore	fireplace	arrowhead
daydream	cookbook	somewhere	headache
goldfish	bookmark	anything	downstairs
jellyfish	playmate	streetcar	upstairs
fishfry	playground	sandbox	bumblebee
doghouse	paperback	popcorn	racetrack
houseboat	wallpaper	corncob	horsefly
housefly	sunburn	oatmeal	wishbone
firefly	sunflower	handlebar	jumpsuit
bodyguard	sunshine	something	everybody

Specific Skills Word Lists (cont.)

Syllable Patterns Word List (pages 112 and 113)
Two-Syllable Words

Short Vowels

vcc	vcv	doubles
listen	magic	yellow
carpet	camel	supper
party	shadow	ladder
bucket	rapid	summer
jacket	shiver	matter
window	travel	rubber
under	visit	banner
sister	edit	worry
forget	metal	hollow
comfort	solid	buzzer
blister	limit	rabbit
bargain	exit	button

Long Vowels

vcv
begin
flavor
lotion
station
repeat
protect
detail
open
final
lazy
delay
robot

Three-Syllable Words

understand	bicycle
elephant	favorite
ornament	submarine
consonant	beautiful
butterfly	popular
umbrella	yesterday
holiday	exciting
tomato	tomorrow
natural	carnival
hamburger	generous

Four-Syllable Words

impossible	secretary
experiment	elevator
contradiction	observation
limitation	unhappily
motivation	calculator
television	disqualify
complication	celebration
invitation	motorcycle
thermometer	comfortable
operation	watermelon

Most Frequently Used English Words

Following is a rank-order listing of the 300 most frequently used words in the English language.

1–50

the	he	at	but	there
of	was	be	not	use
and	for	this	what	an
a	on	have	all	each
to	are	from	were	which
in	as	or	we	she
is	with	one	when	do
you	his	had	your	how
that	they	by	can	their
it	I	word	said	if

51–100

will	some	two	my	find
up	her	more	than	long
other	would	write	first	down
about	make	go	water	day
out	like	see	been	did
many	him	number	call	get
then	into	no	who	come
them	time	way	oil	made
these	has	could	its	may
so	look	people	now	part

101–150

over	live	name	old	too
new	me	good	boy	any
sound	back	sentence	follow	same
take	give	man	also	tell
only	most	think	around	came
little	very	say	where	want
work	after	great	help	show
know	thing	much	through	form
place	our	before	line	three
year	just	mean	right	small

Most Frequently Used
English Words (cont.)

151–200

set	such	land	change	letter
put	because	different	off	mother
end	turn	home	play	answer
does	here	us	spell	found
another	why	move	air	study
well	ask	try	away	still
large	went	kind	animal	learn
must	men	hand	house	should
big	read	picture	point	American
even	need	again	page	world

201–250

high	last	light	along	life
every	school	thought	might	always
near	father	head	close	those
add	deep	under	something	both
food	tree	story	seem	paper
between	never	saw	next	together
own	start	left	hard	got
below	city	don't	open	group
country	earth	few	example	often
plant	eye	while	begin	run

251–300

important	sea	hear	watch	cut
until	began	stop	far	young
children	grow	without	Indian	talk
side	took	second	real	soon
feet	river	later	almost	list
car	four	miss	let	song
mile	carry	idea	above	being
night	state	enough	girl	leave
walk	once	eat	sometimes	family
white	book	face	mountain	it's

Glossary of Language Terms

abbreviation The shortened form of a word. Many abbreviations begin with a capital letter and end with a period.

Examples: **Mrs. Dr. Ave. Dec.**

ABC order To put words into alphabetical order by using their beginning letters.

Example: **ant be candle cost dime**

adjective A word that describes a noun or pronoun. Adjectives tell how many, what kind, which one.

Examples: <u>**Several**</u> **students ride the bus to school.**

Nathan picked up the <u>**hairy**</u> **spider.**

It is your turn to choose the <u>**first**</u> **player.**

adverb A word that describe a verb, adjective, or other adverbs. It tells when, where, and to what extent.

Examples: **The snow has melted** <u>**now.**</u>

The marbles scattered <u>**everywhere.**</u>

Birds sing <u>**sweetly**</u> **in the trees.**

I can <u>**hardly**</u> **wait.**

alphabetize To put words in alphabetical order by using their beginning letters.

Example: **animal butter candle country danger eel**

antonym A word that has the opposite meaning of another word.

Examples: **hot - cold   happy - sad**

apostrophe A mark used in contractions and in the possessive form of a noun.

Examples: **isn't   Sally's book**

articles A kind of adjective that comes before nouns, pronouns, or other adjectives.

They are **a, an,** and **the.**

code A set of symbols or numbers that are used in the place of the existing letters in a word.

Glossary of Language Terms (cont.)

comma

A mark of punctuation used to separate words in a list, to set off a noun of address, to set off an appositive that tells more about a noun just named, after introductory words or phrases, to separate the day of the week from the month and the year, to separate cities and states, and after the greeting and closing of letters.

Examples: **Father bought eggs, milk, bread, and cola.**

Dr. Capp, is your office open today?

Ginny, my cousin, is a good speller.

Today is Monday, October 27, 1999.

I'm going to Austin, Texas, this summer.

Dear Uncle Robert,

Your friend,

command

A sentence that makes a request or orders someone to do something. Also called an imperative sentence.

Examples: **Listen to this, everyone.**

Look at the beautiful rainbow.

Please stop that talking.

common syllable

A letter or group of letters that are found at the beginning or ending of many words. See also prefix and suffix.

Examplse: **mistake**

mister

government

cement

compare

To tell how things are alike.

Example: **Apples and bananas are both fruit.**

compound word

A word that is made by joining two separate words together.

Examplse: **sun light = sunlight**

bare foot = barefoot

compound predicate

A predicate of a sentence that has two or more parts. The parts are joined by the words *or, and,* or *but.*

Examples: **Our class <u>wrote and published the school paper</u>.**

Martha <u>phoned but failed to reach us at home.</u>

compound subject

A subject of a sentence that has two or more parts. The parts are joined by the words *or, and,* or *but.*

Examples: **<u>Beavers and otters</u> swim very well.**

<u>Helen or Stephen</u> will empty the trash tonight.

contraction

A word formed by joining two other words together to make one. An apostrophe is used to show where letter or letters have been taken out.

Examples: **has not = hasn't**

we have = we've

Glossary of Language Terms *(cont.)*

contrast
To tell how things are different.

Example: **Dogs have fur, and birds have feathers.**

declarative
A sentence that makes a statement or tells information. A declarative sentence ends with a period.

Example: **The blue whale is bigger than thirty elephants.**

descriptive paragraph
A group of sentences that describe something. It gives details that tell how something looks, feels, tastes, smells, or sounds.

dialogue
The words that someone says to another when having a conversation. It is shown in writing by using quotation marks.

Example: **The mechanic said, "A nail has caused your flat tire."**

entry
The information given in a dictionary for an entry word.

Example: **frigate (frig it) n.** a fast, medium sized sailing warship of the early 18th and 19th centuries. The frigate carried enough supplies to last six months at sea.

entry word
The words that are entered in a dictionary. Each entry word has information such as its spelling, definition, pronunciation, part of speech, and other forms of the word given in its entry.

exclamatory
A sentence that expresses strong feelings or excitement. It ends in an exclamation mark.

Examples: **What a huge appetite he has!**

                I just can't believe I won the spelling contest!

fact
True information about something that can be proven.

Examples: **The school day begins at 7:50.**

                Mt. Adams is closer to Ashville than Richmond.

future tense
Time that has not yet happened but will in the future. The future tense is usually formed with the helping verb "will" or "shall."

Examples: **The scientist will measure the glacier.**

                I shall meet you for lunch next week.

guide words
Words found at the top of a dictionary page that tell you the first and last words found on that specific page in alphabetical order.

Glossary of Language Terms *(cont.)*

helping verb   A verb that works with the main verb to express action or being. Some common helping verbs are these:

am	be	had	did	might
is	being	can	shall	must
are	been	could	should	were
was	has	do	will	
have	does	would	may	

Examples: **The crowd <u>has</u> left the stadium.**

The fans <u>are</u> walking to their cars.

homophones   Words that are pronounced the same but are spelled differently and have different meanings.

Examples: **plane—plain**

hall—haul

here—hear

imperative   A sentence that makes a request, command, or orders someone to do something.

Examples: **Go sharpen your pencils for the spelling test.**

Please wash and dry the dishes after you have eaten.

interrogative   A sentence that asks a question. An interrogative sentence ends with a question mark.

Example: **Do you know where Mobile, Alabama, is on the map?**

naming part   The part of the sentence that tells who or what the sentence is about. Also called the subject.

Example: **<u>Ice skating</u> is a popular sport in the winter.**

narrative   A paragraph that tells a story about events that happened to the writer or to someone else. It can be real or imaginary.

noun   A word that names a person, place, or thing.

opinion   What a person thinks or how a person feels about something.

Examples: **Green apples are the best.**

Ms. Brown is an excellent math teacher.

paragraph   A group of sentences that tell about one topic.

part of speech   The label given a word according to how it is used in a sentence. Some of the parts of speech are noun, verb, pronoun, adjective, adverb, and preposition.

Glossary of Language Terms *(cont.)*

past tense   Something that has already happened. The past tense of a verb is usually formed by adding "-ed." Some verbs have new words to show past tense.

Examples: **Water <u>poured</u> down the mountainside.**

We <u>saw</u> fireworks from our backyard. (Also see present tense.)

plural   Meaning more than one person, place, or thing. A plural noun is usually formed by adding "-s." Some nouns add "-es" or even have new words to show plural.

Examples: **The <u>cows</u> are grazing in the pasture.**

Father has seven gate <u>passes</u> to the car race.

My <u>feet</u> are killing me!

plural possessive   A plural noun that shows possession or ownership of something. Plural nouns ending in "-s" add an apostrophe (') to show possession. Plural nouns that do not end in "-s" add an apostrophe "-s" ('s).

Examples: **The <u>soldiers'</u> tent protected them from the storm.**

The men's room was closed for cleaning.

possessive   To show that a noun has ownership of possession of something. Most singular nouns add an apostrophe and "-s" ('s) to show possession. Plural nouns ending in -s, add only an apostrophe. Plural nouns that do not end in "-s" add apostrophe "-s" ('s).

Examples: **The <u>cat's</u> tail was caught in the door.**

The <u>teachers'</u> workroom was crowded.

Our <u>child's</u> program begins at 3:00.

predicate   The part of a sentence that tells what the subject does, did, or is doing. The predicate contains a verb.

Examples: **Some airplanes <u>are built to carry army tanks.</u>**

prefix   A letter or group of letters added to the beginning of a word. The prefix changes the meaning of the word. Some common prefixes are these:

dis-   **mis-**   **un-**   **re-**
pre-   **im-**   **in-**

present tense   Something that is happening now.

Examples: **The students study for their science test.**

It is thundering and lightning outside.

Glossary of Language Terms *(cont.)*

present tense   A word that takes the place of a person, place, or thing. Pronouns can be singular or plural.

Example: **Singular**   **Plural**

I, me, mine, my   we, us, our, ours

you, your, yours   you, your, yours

he, she, it, him   they, them

her, his, hers, its   their, theirs

proper noun   The name of a specific person, place, or thing. A proper noun always begins with a capital letter.

Example: **Sally will go to the West Hills Academy in September.**

punctuation   The marks and symbols used in sentences to help the reader understand what is written. Following are some common punctuation marks:

period—.
comma—,
question mark—?
apostrophe—'
quotation marks—" "
exclamation mark—!

question   A sentence that asks something. Also known as an interrogative sentence. A question always ends with a question mark.

Example: **Whose turn is it to walk the dog?**

quotation marks   The punctuation marks put around the words spoken (dialogue) by someone in a sentence.

Example: **"I love your new bicycle," said Bethany.**

sentence   A group of words that express a complete thought. A sentence has a subject and a verb. The four types of sentences are declarative, interrogative, imperative, and exclamatory.

singular possessive   When a single noun shows ownership or possession of something. A singular noun adds an apostrophe and "-s" ('s) to show possession.

Example: **The baker's shop smells wonderful.**

statement   A sentence that tells you information. Also called a declarative sentence. A statement ends with a period.

Example: **Ben was frightened by the storm.**

subject   The part of a sentence that names the person, place, or thing the sentence is telling about.

Example: ***The tulip*** **blooms in late spring and early summer.**

Glossary of Language Terms *(cont.)*

suffix   A letter or group of letters added to the end of a word. A suffix changes the meaning of the word. Following are some suffixes:

-able
-er
-ful
-ive
-less
-ous
-y
-ment
-ness
-ly

syllables   The parts or letter groups heard to make a complete word. Each syllable has one vowel sound but may have several letters. Syllables can be heard as beats or separate parts when saying a word.

Examples: **shady = 2 syllables sha/dy (sha—has a long a sound)**

(dy—has a long e sound)

dynamite = 3 syllables dy/na/mite (dy—has a long i sound)

(na—has a schwa sound)

(mite—has a long i sound)

synonym   A word that has the same or nearly the same meaning as another word.

Example: **small—*little***

ruin—*destroy*

permit—*allow*

telling part   The part of a sentence that tells what the subject does, did, or is doing. The telling part contains a verb. The telling part is called the predicate.

verb   A word that expresses action or state or being. It tells what something does, did, or is doing.

Examples: **action verbs**   **state of being verbs**

action verbs	state of being verbs
build	be
run	is
move	was
carry	am
help	are
swim	were
melt	being
borrowed	been